The Torah

BIBAL™ Study Program 1

The Torah

by

Duane L. Christensen

BIBAL Press
North Richland Hills, Texas

Published by

BIBAL Press
An imprint of D. & F. Scott Publishing, Inc.
P.O. Box 821653
N. Richland Hills, TX 76182
817 788-2280
info@dfscott.com
www.dfscott.com

and

The Institute of International Studies
An agency of BIBAL Corporation
845 Bodega Way
Rodeo, CA 94572
Phone (510) 377-7000   Fax (801) 650-9283
E-mail: dlc@bibal.net
www.bibal.net

Printed in the United States of America

06 05 04 03 02   5 4 3 2 1

Library of Congress Cataloging-in-Publication Data
Christensen, Duane L., 1938-
    The Torah / by Duane L. Christensen.
        p. cm. — (BIBAL study program ; 1)
    ISBN 1-930566-25-5 (pbk. : alk. paper)
    1. Bible. O.T. Pentateuch—Textbooks. I. Title. II. Series.
    BS1227 .C47 2002
    222'.1106—dc21
                                        2002007309

"And I looked, and behold, there were four wheels . . .
(and) the four had the same likeness,
as if a wheel were within a wheel."

[Ezekiel 10:9–10]

The six books in the BIBAL Study Program are dedicated to my six grandchildren:

The Torah	*Benjamin Joseph Clark*
The Former Prophets	*Erin Hilary Clark*
The Latter Prophets	*Stephanie Michelle Clark*
The Writings of the Tanakh	*Timothy Daniel Clark*
Apostolic Writings 1: Gospels and Acts	*Christopher Robert Welin*
Apostolic Writings 2: Epistles and Revelation	*Michael Russell Welin*

"From childhood may you be acquainted with the sacred writings which are able to instruct you for salvation through faith in Messiah Yeshua (Jesus Christ)."
2 Timothy 3:15

Contents

Preface—A Personal Note to the Reader   xi

1. The Book of Genesis   1
   Genesis and the Primary History (Torah and Former Prophets)   1
   Genesis 1-11 as Introduction to the Bible   3
   Reading the Book of Genesis from the Center   7
   Genesis 1-11 and the Book of Jonah: from Torah to Latter Prophets   15
   Genesis and the Bible as a Whole   18

2. The Book of Exodus   23
   Exodus and the Wars of Yahweh   23
   Moses as Leader in Ancient Israel   26
   Reading the Book of Exodus from the Center   28
   The Tabernacle in the Religion of Israel   43
   Passover within the Canonical Process   48

3. The Book of Leviticus   53
   Yahweh's Hidden Presence in Leviticus and the Torah   53
   The Tabernacle in the Book of Leviticus   55
   Reading the Book of Leviticus from the Center   57
   Holiness in the Book of Leviticus   62
   Exodus and Leviticus as a Literary Unit   64

4. The Book of Numbers   69
   The Book of Numbers within the Torah   69
   The Wilderness Encampment—Levites as Guards of the Tabernacle   71
   Reading the Book of Numbers from the Center   73
   Numbers and the "Book of the Wars of Yahweh" (Num 21:14)   79
   Numbers within the Primary History—Evidence for a "Master Editor"   80

5. The Book of Deuteronomy   85
   Deuteronomy as the Center of the Canonical Process   85
   The Musical Composition of Deuteronomy   88
   Reading the Book of Deuteronomy from the Center   91
   The Numerical Composition of Deuteronomy   109
   Law and Narrative in the Bible   114

Answers to Concept Checks   119
The BIBAL™ Study Program   125

Preface—A Personal Note to the Reader

Many of us have a burning desire to feel at home with the Bible—to know its contents in depth. This textbook is designed to help you achieve fluency in your use of the Bible. This particular book focuses on the *Torah*, which is the first and most important section of the canon of the Tanakh (Old Testament). In Jewish tradition, it is the "canon within the canon."

The canon of sacred Scripture, as Messiah Yeshua (Jesus Christ) and His followers in the first century knew it, is divided into four parts:

Torah	Genesis, Exodus, Leviticus, Numbers, Deuteronomy
Former Prophets	Joshua, Judges, 1–2 Samuel, 1–2 Kings
Latter Prophets	Isaiah, Jeremiah, Ezekiel, the Twelve (Minor Prophets)
Writings	Psalms, Job, Proverbs, Festal Scrolls (Ruth, Song of Songs, Ecclesiastes, Lamentations, Esther), Daniel, Ezra, Nehemiah, 1–2 Chronicles

The Second Testament (New Testament) was added as a fifth section of the canon to complete the Bible, in what we call the *COMPLETED TANAKH*.[1]

This book is one of six textbooks for the "Core Courses" of the BIBAL Study Program, which is designed to help you establish a solid foundation so that you can master the contents of the Bible as a whole. The courses are independent and need not be taken in any particular sequence. We suggest, however, that you take either or both of the two introductory courses first, if possible. This will enable you to get the most possible from each of the remaining courses. The eight courses in the BIBAL Study Program, which are described in detail at the end of this book, are as follows:

Introduction to the Bible
The Bible as a Whole

The Torah
The Former Prophets
The Latter Prophets
The Writings of the Tanakh
Apostolic Writings I: The Gospels and Acts
Apostolic Writings II: The Epistles and Revelation

My prayers are with you as you progress toward fluency in your personal use of the Bible.

Agape and shalom,

Dr. Duane L. Christensen

---

1 The word Tanakh is an acronym, which refers to the Bible. The word is made up of the initial letter from the Hebrew name of the three sections of the canon: Torah, Prophets (*Nevi'im*), and Writings (*Kethuvim*)—TaNaKh.

1

The Book of Genesis

Contents

A. Genesis and the Primary History (Torah and Former Prophets)
B. Genesis 1–11 as Introduction to the Bible
C. Reading the Book of Genesis from the Center
D. Genesis 1–11 and the Book of Jonah—from Torah to Latter Prophets
E. Genesis and the Bible as a Whole

Objectives

When this chapter is completed, the student should be able to:

♦ Discuss the function of Genesis 1–11 within the canonical process

♦ Explain the significance of the change in name from Abram to Abraham

♦ Discuss the role of Isaac in the narrative structure of Genesis

♦ Discuss the role of the "Matriarchs" in Genesis

♦ Explain why the term "Joseph Story" is not adequate to describe Genesis 37–50

♦ Discuss the relationship between Genesis 1–11 and the book of Jonah

A. Genesis and the Primary History (Torah and Former Prophets)

In Jewish tradition the book of Genesis is called בראשית (pronounced *Be-re'sheet*), the first word of the Hebrew text, which may be translated "In the beginning." This is apropos for Genesis is a book about beginnings, and Genesis 1–11 is the introduction to all that follows in the "Completed Tanakh" (First and Second Testament). Genesis is the first of five books commonly called the Torah, *Chumash*, the Pentateuch (literally, "five-fold vessel"), the five books of Moses, or simply the Law.

A thumbnail sketch of the contents of the Torah may be represented as follows:

Genesis	Israel's origin and early years	Beginnings
Exodus	Israel's deliverance from bondage in Egypt	Deliverance
Leviticus	Israel's worship, directed by the Levites	Legislation
Numbers	Israel's wilderness wandering in the Sinai Peninsula	Testing
Deuteronomy	Israel awaiting entrance into the land of Canaan	Preparation

The Torah is the record of God's revelation in history and his lordship over history. It testifies both to Israel's response and to her failure to respond. It witnesses to God's holiness, which separates him from human beings, and his gracious love, which binds him to them on his terms.

Though the "Moses Story" (Exodus through Deuteronomy) is the beginning of the canonical process from an historical point of view, it constitutes the second chapter of God's story in human history within the Tanakh (Hebrew Bible). The first chapter is the book of Genesis, which functions as the introduction to the Primary History (Torah and Former Prophets). This larger body of material may be outlined in a nested menorah pattern, as follows:

The Primary History in a Menorah Pattern	*Genesis–2 Kings*
A Primeval history: from Creation to dispersion of the nations	Genesis 1–11
B Land promise given to Abraham, Isaac, and Jacob	12–50
C Egypt judged—plagues and institution of Passover	Exod 1:1–12:36
X **Exodus and Eisodus—the wars of Yahweh**	**Exod 12:37–Josh 4**
C´ Canaan conquered—observance of Passover	Joshua 5–12
B´ Land promise fulfilled—allotment of the Promised Land	13–24
A´ Special History: "Joseph" and Judah among the nations	Judges–2 Kings

2^(nd) *Level: Exodus and Eisodus—the Wars of Yahweh*	*Exod 12:37–Josh 4:24*
A Exodus from Egypt—crossing *Yam Suf* (Sea of Reeds)	Exod 12:37–14:31
B Song of Moses at the crossing of the Sea	15:1–21
C Wilderness wandering under leadership of Moses	15:22–18:27
X **Covenant and Theophany at Mount Sinai**	Exod 19:1–Num 10:10
C´ Wilderness wandering and transfer of leadership	Num 10:11–Deut 31:30
B´ Song of Moses in Moab; blessing and death of Moses	Deuteronomy 32–34
A´ Eisodus (entry) into Canaan—crossing the Jordan River	Joshua 1–4

3^(rd) *Level: Covenant and Theophany at Mount Sinai*	*Exod 19:1–Num 10:10*
A Covenant between God and Israel ratified and regulated	Exod 19:1–24:18
B Tabernacle planned	25:1–31:18
C Covenant broken—Golden Calf incident	32:1–35
X **Theophany on Sinai—the promised presence**	33:1–23
C´ Covenant renewed	34:1–35
B´ Tabernacle built	35:1–40:38
A´ Covenant regulations	Lev 1:1–Num 10:10

Though it is proper to think of the Torah as a literary unit within the Tanakh, it is also important to remember that it is an integral part of all that follows—in both testaments. The book of Deuteronomy, in particular, functions as a bridge connecting the Torah and the Former Prophets.

Genesis	Exodus	Joshua	Judges
	Deuteronomy		
Leviticus	Numbers	Samuel	Kings

The contents of the Former Prophets may be outlined in a menorah pattern, as follows:

The Former Prophets in a Menorah Pattern   *Joshua–2 Kings*
A Taking the land under charismatic leadership   Joshua
B   Possessing the land under charismatic judges   Judges
C   Possessing the land under charismatic kings (Saul and David)   1 Samuel
X   **The kingdom of David established**   2 Sam 1:1–2:4a
C´   Possessing the land under a dynastic king (David)   2 Samuel
B´ Possessing the land under dynastic kings (Solomon to Ahab)   1 Kings
A´ Loss of the land under monarchic leadership   2 Kings

In short, the epic story, which begins with the Exodus from Egypt under Moses and the Eisodus into the Promised Land under Joshua, culminates in the establishment of the kingdom of David.

Concept Check #1

What is the structural center of the so-called "Primary History"?
Check your answer at the back of this book.

B. Genesis 1–11 as Introduction to the Bible

As the introduction to the Bible as a whole, Genesis 1–11 is a remarkable work of literary art that cannot be reduced to any single structure. These eleven chapters constitute the first two of fifty-four weekly portions (Parashoth) in the annual cycle of readings from the Torah in traditional Jewish worship. One of the more useful readings of the Primeval History may be outlined as follows:

Parashoth 1–2: The Primeval History in a Menorah Pattern—#1   *Genesis 1–11*
A   Adam and Eve—the story of creation   1:1–3:21
B   Expulsion from the Garden of Eden   3:22–4:26
C   Generations of Adam and sons   5:1–32
X   **Noah and the flood—a new creation**   6:1–9:29
C´   Generations of Noah and sons   10:1–26
B´ Dispersion—the story of the Tower of Babel   11:1–9
A´ Abram and Sarai—beginning of a new story   11:10–32

A primary function of Genesis 1–11 is to take the reader from the story of Adam and Eve to that of Abram and Sarai, on route to the land of Canaan (11:31). To get there, we move from Creation (Adam), to a new creation (Noah), to the advent of a special creation—a covenant people who are the descendants of a barren woman (11:30). The opening account of the Creation Story (Genesis 1–4), which includes the account of Adam and his three sons (Cain, Abel, and Seth), is set over against the dispersion of human beings among the people groups of antiquity in the story of the Tower of Babel.

This latter story is preceded by the account of Noah and his three sons: Shem, Ham, and Japheth (Genesis 10–11). Within this structure we find a reference to Enoch, a man who "walked with God" (Gen 5:22), and the elaborate story of Noah who also "walked with God" (Gen 6:9). These are the only two individuals in Genesis whose relationship with God is described in this terminology.

Genesis 1–11 also functions as the introduction to more distant texts in the Torah (Deut 31:2 and 34:7), and the Writings (Job 1–2 and Prov 8:22–31), as careful reflection on the details of the following menorah pattern suggests:

Parashoth 1–2: The Primeval History in a Menorah Pattern—#2   *Genesis 1–11*

A   Story of Creation (ending with Adam's three sons)   1:1–4:26
B   From Adam to Noah: Enoch ("walked with God"—5:22)   5:1–32
C   Sons of God take daughters of *ha'adam* as wives   6:1–2
X   **Yahweh speaks—a "riddle in the middle"**   6:3
C´   Sons of God and daughters of *ha'adam* breed giants   6:4
B´   Story of Noah (who "walked with God"—6:9)   6:5–9:29
A´ Story of Dispersion (starting with Noah's three sons)   10:1–11:32

When Yahweh says, "My spirit shall not abide in *ha'adam* forever . . . their days shall be one hundred and twenty years" (6:3), the meaning is not at all clear. The structure poses a "riddle in the middle" to the reader, who is startled by the sudden reference to what looks on the surface like mythology—as "sons of God" marry "daughters of Adam" to produce the giants of old (the Nephilim, 6:4).

It is possible to interpret the text as a limit of one hundred and twenty years, and then God will send final judgment in the Great Flood. At the same time, the curious word *beshaggam* in the middle of this verse has at least two meanings. Of the two most obvious possibilities, the traditional rendering "in that also" *ha'adam* is flesh (i.e., mortal) is followed by most translators, ancient and modern. That same word, however, may also be translated "because of their going astray," with the variant reading, which appears in some Hebrew manuscripts. The only difference between the two readings is the length of the vowel in the final syllable of the word *beshaggam*. At the same time, however, the reference to a limitation of one hundred and twenty years calls attention to the two references to the death of Moses in Deut 31:2 and 34:7 at the age of 120. These two verses are the only other places in the entire Bible where the number 120 appears as a limitation in life span. Moses died because he was a hundred and twenty years old—but he did not die because he was physically worn out. "His eye was not dim, nor his natural force abated" (Deut 34:7, KJV). He died because he reached the limit God had set for him, namely the limit of one hundred and twenty years, which is anticipated in the "riddle in the middle" of Gen 6:3. In the annual cycle of fifty-four weekly portions (Parashoth) of Torah readings in the Jewish synagogue, Deut 34:7 and Gen 6:3 are read in consecutive weeks. Parashah 54 (Deut 33:1–34:12) is recited on Simchat Torah, followed by the reading of Parashah 1 (Gen 1:1–6:8).

Another way of looking at Genesis 1–11, with the story of Noah at the center, is to focus attention on the repeated occurrences of the words, "These are the generations of . . ." (especially in 2:4, 6:9, 10:1, and 11:10).

Parashoth 1–2: The Primeval History in a Menorah Pattern—#3   *Genesis 1–11*

A Creation in seven days   1:1–2:3
B   The *generations* of heaven and earth: Adam and Eve + three sons   2:4–4:26
C   Genealogy: list of *descendants* from Adam through Noah   5:1–32
X   Noah and the flood—a new creation   6:1–9:28
C´   Genealogy: the *descendants* of Noah's three sons [70 nations]   10:1–31
B´ The *generations* of Noah's three sons and the Tower of Babel   10:32–11:9
A´ Election in ten *generations*: from Shem to Terah (Abram's father)   11:10–32

In this menorah pattern, the outside frame moves from creation of the entire universe ("heaven and earth") and the story of Adam and Eve (1:1–3:3), to God's "election" of a single human couple in the person of Abram and Sarai (11:10–32). In between we find two parallel stories: that of "Adam and sons" and the story of "Noah and sons." There are three sons in each instance; and each series is in turn expanded into a genealogical list of descendants. We move from Adam to Noah and his three sons (in Genesis 5), and from Noah and his three sons to the so-called "Table of Nations" (in Genesis 10), which presents a record of the seventy nations of antiquity. According to the genealogies of the sons of Noah these nations "spread abroad on the face of the earth after the flood" (Gen 10:32).

The seven occurrences of the *toledot* formula in Genesis 1–11, which is translated "(these are) the *generations* of" or "(these are) the *descendants* of," may be outlined in a menorah pattern, as follows:

A These are the *descendants* of heaven and earth   Gen 2:4
B   This is the account of the *descendants* of Adam   Gen 5:1
C   These are the *descendants* of Noah   Gen 6:9
X   The descendants of Noah's sons: Shem, Ham and Japheth   Gen 10:1
C´   The families of Noah's sons according to their *descendants*   Gen 10:32
B´ These are the *descendants* of Shem [ancestor of the "Semites"]   Gen 11:10
A´ These are the *descendants* of Terah (father of Abram)   Gen 11:27

The outermost frame moves from the creation of heaven and earth to election, in God's choice of a single man from whom to accomplish his work among the nations. At the same time, it is important to note that the concentric structure converges on the descendants of Noah's three sons, which constitute the seventy nations of antiquity—i.e., all human beings. Even before God declares to Abram that all the families of the earth will be blessed through him (Gen 12:3), God's plans already embrace the whole world.

The reference to the "sons of God" in Gen 6:1–4 should be interpreted in relation to the story of Job, where "the sons of God" come to present themselves before Yahweh, and Satan comes also among them (Job 1:6). In like manner, the figure of Lady Wisdom takes her place as God's first act of creation, and his "delight," before Gen 1:1 (cf. Prov 8:22–31). These texts are discussed later in the BIBAL Study Program, in *The Writings of the Tanakh*.

Most students of the Bible note a major shift in literary structure between Genesis 11 and 12. One way of showing this fact is the following diagram:

Genesis 1–11:   **God Dealing with the Human Race**
Four great events   [Creation ⇒ Fall ⇒ Flood + Tower of Babel]
Human failure
God preparing for the covenant with Abraham
~ ~

Genesis 12–50:   **God Dealing with a Single People**
Four great individuals [Abram/Abraham ⇒ Isaac ⇒ Jacob/Israel + Joseph & Judah]
God preserving the covenant with Abraham

In this reading, the key concept for understanding Genesis is the covenant with Abraham. The book of Genesis is in two major parts, which are similar in structure. On the one hand, Genesis 1–11 deals with all the people of the world. Here God is preparing the way for establishing his covenant with Abraham. The focus is on human failure and the need for God's grace. Genesis 12–50 narrows the focus to a single people and God's covenant of grace with Abraham through whom all the nations of the earth will ultimately be blessed (Gen 18:18).

Each of these two major sections is in four parts, the first three of which form a literary unit. The story of the flood concludes with God's covenant with Noah in which the original words addressed to Adam in Gen 1:28 are repeated: "Be fruitful and multiply, and fill the earth" (Gen 9:1). The narrative moves from creation (Adam) to a renewal of creation (Noah) and concludes with a story of dispersion in the account of the Tower of Babel (Genesis 11). Genesis 12–50 presents the account of the three Patriarchs (Abraham, Isaac and Jacob), which moves from father (Abram/Abraham) to grandson (Jacob/Israel), both of whom have their names changed at decisive moments in the narrative. The concluding story is different with its focus on Joseph and Judah among the twelve sons of Jacob (Genesis 37–50).

Concept Check #2
In light of the structures presented here, what is the central message of Genesis 1–11?
Check your answer at the back of this book.

C. Reading the Book of Genesis from the Center

One way of looking at the structure of Genesis is to outline the book in a nested menorah pattern with its focus on Isaac blessing his two sons, Jacob and Esau.

The Book of Genesis in a Menorah Pattern	*Genesis 1–50*
A Primeval history	1:1–11:32
B Abram/Abraham narrative cycle	12:1–25:18
C Jacob and Esau—Isaac seeks refuge in Philistia (Gerar)	25:19–26:34
X **Isaac blesses Jacob and Esau**	27:1–28:4
C´ Jacob and Esau—Jacob seeks refuge in Paddan-aram	28:5–9
B´ Jacob/Israel and Esau/Edom narrative cycle	28:10–35:43
A´ Special History (foreshadowed): focus on Joseph and Judah	37:1–50:26

2ⁿᵈ Level Menorah: Isaac Blesses Jacob and Esau	*Gen 27:1–28:4*
A Isaac's request—that Esau bring him "savory food"	27:1–4
B Rebekah instructs Jacob and assists him in deceiving Isaac	27:5–26
C Isaac blesses Jacob thinking he is blessing Esau	27:27–29
X **Esau brings "savory food" to receive Isaac's blessing**	27:30–38
C´ Isaac blesses Esau (inverting words of Jacob's blessing)	27:39–40
B´ Rebekah instructs Jacob to flee Esau's wrath	27:41–45
A´ Isaac's request—that Jacob take a wife in Paddan-aram	27:46–28:4

The menorah pattern here focuses on the blessing of both Jacob and Esau, which they receive from their father Isaac. The two blessings appear at the structural center of the book of Genesis, framing the account of the arrival of Esau with the savory food his father had requested (Gen 27:30–38). In the center of this passage we find the words of Isaac who is trembling violently as he tells Esau that he has just blessed another in his place—"and he shall be blessed" (27:35). The words spoken cannot be retracted. Isaac manages to bless his son Esau as well, but the very words contain an inversion of the blessing already given to Jacob (cf. 27:28 and 27:39).

1. The Twelve Parashoth in the Book of Genesis

In traditional Jewish worship, the Torah is divided into fifty-four weekly portions (Parashoth). These readings are presented in an annual cycle, which begins and ends each year on Simchat Torah ("Joy of the Torah"). Study of the twelve Parashoth in Genesis suggests that the scribes in antiquity divided the book in half—into two "wheels of the same likeness," as follows:

Parashoth 1–4: From Creation to the Akedah (Binding of Isaac)	*Genesis 1–22*
A Primeval history—from Adam to Abram and Nahor {Abram's brother}	1:1–11:26
B Abram and Sarai—Abram in land of Egypt; expulsion of Hagar	11:27–16:5
C Birth of Ishmael {Abram 86 years old}	16:6–15
X **Covenant of circumcision with Abram/Abraham**	17:1–27
C´ Birth of Isaac—announced and fulfilled {Abraham 100 years old}	18:1–21:7
B´ Abraham and Sarah—expulsion of Hagar; Abraham in land of Philistines	21:8–34
A´ Binding of Isaac (*Akedah*) and genealogy of Nahor {Abraham's brother}	22:1–24

Parashoth 5–12: Death of the Ancestors—from Sarah to Joseph   *Genesis 23–50*

A   Sarah's death (age 127) to burial and death of Abraham (age 175)   23:1–25:11
B   Ishmael and Isaac (genealogies)   25:12–26
C   Jacob and Esau (narrative)—rivalry and estrangement   25:27–35:26
X   **Death of Isaac (age 180)**   35:27–29
C´   Esau (genealogy)—Edomite lists   36:1–42
B´   Joseph and Judah (narrative)—descent into Egypt   37:1–48:22
A´ Jacob's death (age 147); burial and death of Joseph (age 110)   49:1–50:26

The Primeval History in Genesis 1–11 closes with a brief note on the descendants of Terah, the father of Abram, Nahor and Haran (11:26). Nahor is not mentioned again until Gen 22:20, where the children of Nahor are listed in a unit that functions as the second half of an envelope around the story of Abram/Abraham. That story reaches its climax in the mysterious episode in which Abraham is commanded by God to offer his son Isaac as a burnt offering on Mount Moriah, a story called the *Akedah* (the "binding" of Isaac).

The center of the first half of Genesis is the covenant of circumcision, which El Shaddai establishes with Abram (17:1–14). This is the moment God changes Abram's name to Abraham ("father of a multitude," 17:4). On one side, we find the story of Abram and Sarai, which reaches its climax in the expulsion of the pregnant Hagar, Sarai's maid, followed by the birth of Ishmael as Abram's long awaited son by Hagar (16:1–15). On the other side, we have the narrative about Abraham and Sarah, which reaches another high point in the birth of Isaac to Sarah in her old age, and the expulsion of Ishmael and Hagar from Abraham's household (21:1–21).

Ancient scribes also appear to have divided Genesis into four major sections, each of which may be outlined in similar nested menorah patterns—or "four wheels of the same likeness."

A   Primeval History   Genesis 1–11   Parashoth 1–2
B   Abram/Abraham narrative cycle   Genesis 12–22   Parashoth 3–4
B´   Jacob/Israel and Esau/Edom cycle   Genesis 23–36   Parashoth 5–8
A´ Special History (Joseph and Judah) foreshadowed Genesis 37–50   Parashoth 9–12

The first "wheel" (Genesis 1–11) in this chiastic structure is discussed in the previous section of this chapter (see section B, "Genesis 1–11as Introduction to the Bible").

a. The Abram/Abraham Narrative Cycle (Genesis 12–22)

The content of the Abram/Abraham narrative cycle in Genesis 12–22 may be outlined in a three-part series of nested menorah patterns:

Parashoth 3–4: The Abram/Abraham Narrative Cycle   *Gen 11:27–22:24*

A   Genealogy of Terah (Abraham's father)   11:27–32
B   Start of Abram's spiritual odyssey (Abraham's call)   12:1–5
C   Building of altars in the Promised Land (at Shechem)   12:6–9
X   **Abram/Abraham among foreign peoples**   12:10–21:34
C´   Building of an altar on Mount Moriah to sacrifice Isaac   22:1–9
B´   Climax of Abraham's spiritual odyssey (the *Akedah*)   22:10–19
A´ Genealogy of Nahor (Abraham's brother)   22:20–24

2nd *Level Menorah: Abra(ha)m among Foreign Peoples*   *Gen 12:10–21:34*

A   Sarai's ordeal in a foreign palace; Abram and Lot part   12:10–13:18
B   Abram comes to the rescue of Sodom and Lot   14:1–24
C   Covenant of sacrifice with Abram (and Sarai)   15:1–21
X   **Covenant of circumcision with Abraham (name changed)**   16:1–17:27
C´   A son promised to Abraham and Sarah   18:1–15
B´   Abraham comes to the rescue of Sodom and Lot   18:16–19:38
A´ Sarah's ordeal in a foreign palace; Abraham and Ishmael part   20:1–21:34

3rd *Level Menorah: Covenant of Circumcision with Abraham*   *Genesis 16–17*

A   Hagar (with Ishmael) driven out of Abram's house   16:1–10
B   Birth of Ishmael announced by an angel   16:11–16
C   Yahweh speaks: "I will make my covenant between you and me"   17:1–2
X   **Abram's name changed to Abraham—"father of many nations"**   17:3–8
C´   Elohim speaks: "Every male among you shall be circumcised"   17:9–14
B´   Birth of Isaac announced by God   17:15–19
A´ Ishmael included in the covenant of circumcision   17:20–27

This structure presents the life story of Abraham, describing his journeys and places of worship, promises from and covenants with God, dealings with other peoples in the region, and domestic life. The focus of attention is the all-important question of an heir to Abraham through whom God's covenant promise is to be implemented—and the status of his two sons, Ishmael and Isaac. In the center of this structure, the names of Abram and Sarai are changed to Abraham and Sarah, and the rite of circumcision is instituted as a sign of God's covenant with his chosen people.

b. The Jacob/Israel and Esau/Edom Narrative Cycle (Genesis 23–36)

The third "wheel," which focuses on both Jacob and Esau in Genesis 23–36, may be outlined in another nested menorah pattern, as follows:

Parashoth 5–8: From the Death of Sarah to the Death of Isaac   *Genesis 23–36*

A   Death of Sarah and Abraham and the descendants of Ishmael   23:1–25:18
B   Rivalry between Jacob and Esau—Jacob's journey to Haran   25:19–28:9
C   Jacob's dream at Bethel   28:10–22
X   **Jacob and his family in Haran—in the house of Laban**   29:1–31:55
C´   Jacob wrestles with an angel at the Jabbok—his name changed   32:1–32
B´   Esau and Jacob are reconciled—Jacob's journey to Hebron   33:1–35:27
A´ Death of Isaac and the descendants of Esau   35:28–36:43

2nd *Level Menorah: Jacob and His Family in Haran*   *Genesis 29–31*

A   Jacob arrives at Haran—he meets Rachel at the well   29:1–14
B   Jacob marries Laban's daughters Leah and Rachel   29:15–30
C   Jacob's wife Leah (and concubines) is fertile: ten sons and a daughter   29:31–30:24
X   **Birth of Joseph to Rachel—"May Yahweh add another"**   30:25–26
C´   Jacob's flocks are fertile at the expense of Laban   30:27–43
B´   Jacob leaves Haran with family and flocks—covenant with Laban   31:1–54
A´ Laban returns to Haran   31:55

The focus of attention here narrows to the conflict between Jacob and Esau, and then to Jacob's twenty years in Haran during which eleven of his twelve sons (the tribes of Israel) are born. At the center, the focus is on the birth of Joseph whose name is interpreted as a foreshadowing of the coming birth of his younger brother Benjamin—the only one of the twelve to be born in the Promised Land.

The account of Benjamin's birth appears within the story of Jacob's journey from the Jabbok River to Hebron, which may be outlined in a menorah pattern:

Jacob's Journey "Home" to Hebron and the Birth of Benjamin   *33:1–35:27*
A   Jacob and Esau are reconciled   33:1–17
B   Jacob at Shechem   33:18–20
C   Shechem rapes Dinah—revenge of Levi and Simeon   34:1–31
X   **Jacob's journey to Mamre and birth of Benjamin**   35:1–21
C´   Reuben has sex with Bilhah his father's concubine   35:22a
B´   Jacob and his twelve sons at Hebron—death of Isaac   35:22b–29a
A´ Isaac is buried by Esau and Jacob   35:29b

The outermost frame here moves from the reconciliation of the estranged brothers, Jacob and Esau (33:1–17), to the burial of their father Isaac in which both brothers participate together (35:29b). The innermost frame moves from the story of the rape of Dinah (Genesis 34), to the brief note on Reuben's illicit relationship with his father's concubine (35:22a). And in the center, near the conclusion of Jacob's journey "home," we find the account of the birth of Benjamin and the burial of his mother Rachel who died in childbirth near the town of Bethlehem (35:1–21).

Within the third "wheel" (Genesis 23–36), we find a "wheel within a wheel" that deals with episodes in the life of Isaac's younger son Jacob (Israel) in relation to his twin brother Esau (Edom). Before their birth, God reveals to his mother Rebekah that she has "two nations in her womb" and "the elder shall serve the younger" (Gen 25:23). The rivalry between the brothers is bitter, to the point that Jacob must take refuge from Esau's anger in another country. Eventually Jacob and Esau are reconciled; but in the twenty years that intervene, much happens to set the stage for what follows. Jacob (Israel) has eleven sons and a daughter (Dinah) in the course of seven years who are born in Paddan-aram in Mesopotamia. Another son, Benjamin, is born later in the land of Canaan, after Jacob's ordeal at the Jabbok River (Genesis 32), during which his name is changed to Israel. Benjamin's mother Rachel dies in childbirth and is buried near Bethlehem (Gen 35:18–20). The content of this narrative cycle may be outlined in a nested menorah pattern:

The Jacob/Israel Narrative Cycle in a Menorah Pattern   *Gen 25:7–35:29*
A   Death of Abraham (175) and Ishmael (137)   25:7–18
B   Rebekah's struggle in childbirth, birth of Jacob and Esau   25:19–34
C   Interlude: Rebekah in a foreign palace; pact with foreigners   26:1–35
X   **Conflict between Jacob and Esau**   27:1–33:20
C´   Interlude: Dinah in a foreign palace; pact with foreigners   34:1–31
B´   Rachel's struggle in childbirth, birth of Benjamin   35:1–26
A´ Death of Isaac (180)   35:27–29

2nd *Level Menorah: Conflict between Jacob and Esau*	*Genesis 27–33*

2nd *Level Menorah: Conflict between Jacob and Esau*	*Genesis 27–33*
A Isaac blesses Jacob and Esau—Esau plans to kill Jacob	27:1–46
B Jacob fears Esau and flees to Mesopotamia	28:1–9
C Jacob encounters angels of God at Bethel—Jacob's dream	28:10–22
X **Jacob spends twenty years in Haran with his uncle Laban**	29:1–31:55
C´ Jacob encounters angels of God at Mahanaim	32:1–2
B´ Jacob fears Esau and tries to appease him—Jacob wrestles with God	32:3–32
A´ Jacob and Esau meet after twenty years—their conflict is resolved	33:1–20

After cheating Esau out of his blessing, Jacob travels to the home of his uncle Laban in distant Haran, where Jacob builds a family and acquires considerable wealth.

c. Jacob's Twelve Sons with Focus on Joseph and Judah (Genesis 37–50)

The fourth "wheel" in the concentric structure of Genesis, which is often referred to as the Joseph Story, may also be outlined in a nested menorah pattern:

Parashoth 9–12: Story of Jacob's Twelve Sons (Tribes of Israel)	*Genesis 37–50*
A Joseph and his brothers—Jacob and Joseph part company	37:1–36
B Interlude: story of Judah and Tamar—Joseph not present	38:1–30
C Reversal: Joseph guilty—Potiphar's wife innocent	39:1–23
X **Joseph and his brothers in Egypt**	40:1–47:27
C´ Reversal: Ephraim firstborn—Manasseh secondborn	47:28–48:22
B´ Interlude: blessing Jacob—Joseph nominally present	49:1–28
A´ Joseph and his brothers—Jacob and Joseph part company (in death)	49:29–50:26

2nd *Level Menorah: Joseph and His Brothers in Egypt*	*Gen 40:1–47:27*
A Joseph a hero in Egypt	40:1–41:57
B Joseph's brothers make two trips to Egypt—in search of food	42:1–43:34
C Final test: Joseph detains Benjamin	44:1–17
X **Judah's speech: "(Keep me) in place of the boy"**	44:18–34
C´ Conclusion of the test: Joseph reveals himself	45:1–28
B´ The story of the migration to Egypt is told twice	46:1–47:12
A´ Joseph a hero in Egypt	47:13–27

The focus of attention here is on the twelve sons of Jacob (Israel). Though Joseph is the dominant figure in the story, Judah also plays an important role, particularly in his remarkable speech in the structural center (Gen 44:18–34). Joseph is not presented as a patriarch together with Abraham, Isaac, and Jacob. He is merely one of the twelve sons of Jacob/Israel—and the father of two Israelite tribes, Ephraim and Manasseh, which produce some of Israel's most important leaders (Joshua, Gideon, and Samuel) in the era from Moses to David.

Properly speaking, the story of Joseph is not a story about Joseph alone, but about all twelve sons of Jacob, with its focus on Joseph and Judah. The story foreshadows the role that the tribes of Judah, and "Joseph" (i.e., Ephraim and Manasseh) will play in centuries to come. In particular, a scion of the tribe of Judah, in the person of David, will take center stage at a later point in the unfolding drama of the Bible. It is interesting to note that it is Judah who suggests that his younger brother Joseph be sold into slavery in the first place (Gen 37:26–28). He apparently learns his lesson well; for this time, when his youngest brother Benjamin faces a similar fate, Judah volunteers to take his place in slavery (Gen 44:33).

Many students of the Bible have puzzled over the placing of the story of Judah and Tamar in Genesis 38 after the first chapter in the so-called Joseph Story. One of the reasons becomes evident in the structural design of the whole. The birth of the twins, Perez and Zerah, to Judah through his daughter-in-law Tamar is significant because King David comes from the line of Perez (cf. Ruth 3:11–13).

Like the story of Tamar in Genesis 38, the story of Ruth also turns on the theme of the levirate obligation in the law of Deut 25:5–10. In the "Deathbed Blessing of Jacob" in Genesis 49, which makes up the corresponding section in the above structural design, Judah plays a dominant role in ways that foreshadow, once again, the kingdom of David to come:

> The scepter shall not depart from Judah
>   nor the ruler's staff from between his feet;
> Until tribute comes to him and the obedience of the peoples is his.
> Binding his foal to the vine and his donkey's colt to the choice vine;
> He washes his garments in wine and his robe in the blood of grapes;
> His eyes are darker than wine
>   and his teeth whiter than milk. [Gen 49:10–12]

The imagery of this poem appears again in a much later context, where a scion of David (and Judah) makes his "triumphal entry" into the city of Jerusalem—with Zion's king "coming, sitting on a donkey's colt" (John 12:15; see also Matt 21:15 and Zech 9:9). This event sets the stage for the institution of the "Lord's Supper" and its "blood of grapes" that washes garments stained in sin to make them whiter than snow. The structure of Genesis as a whole reinforces this conclusion, as careful study of the figure of Isaac in the concentric structure of Genesis reveals.

2. Story of Ishmael and Isaac—Putting a Wheel within the Four Wheels

Though the twelve Parashoth in Genesis present a four-part structure of the book, the story of Isaac must be added as a third Patriarch, along with Abraham and his grandson Jacob. The end result may be diagrammed as follows:

The Book of Genesis in Five Parts	*Genesis 1–50*
A Primeval history—from Adam to Abram	1:1–11:32
B Abram/Abraham cycle (with Sarai/Sarah)	12:1–25:11
X Ishmael and Isaac—promised sons of God's covenant	16:1–35:29
B´ Jacob/Israel (and Esau/Edom) cycle	25:19–49:43
A´ Special History (foreshadowed); focus on Joseph and Judah	37:1–50:26

The story of Isaac in Genesis is not a narrative cycle like that of Abram/Abraham and Jacob/Israel. It is contained within the body of these two adjoining narrative cycles and is closely connected with the story of his elder half-brother Ishmael.

The story of Ishmael may be outlined in a menorah pattern, as follows:

The Story of Ishmael in a Menorah Pattern — Gen 16:1–25:18

A Birth of Ishmael to Hagar, Sarai's maid	16:1–15
B Covenant of circumcision includes Ishmael	17:1–27
C Abraham and the birth of Isaac—Ishmael is sent away	18:1–21:34
X The *Akedah*—in which tradition includes Ishmael	22:1–19
C´ Abraham after the *Akedah*—buried by Isaac and Ishmael	22:20–25:11
B´ Descendants of Ishmael	25:12–16
A´ Death of Ishmael at 137 years of age	25:17–18

Jewish tradition places Ishmael in the story of the *Akedah* (binding of Isaac), along with Eliezer of Damascus (15:2); for the two young men that Abraham leaves with his donkey as he and his son Isaac ascend Mount Moriah are identified as Abraham's two prior heirs—Eliezer and Ishmael. Muslim tradition goes much further, for there it is Ishmael who is the intended sacrificial victim and not Isaac.

Ishmael plays a peculiar role in the Bible, along with Hagar his mother, who enjoys the distinction of being the only woman in Genesis 12–50 to whom God communicates directly on two occasions. In the first instance, the angel of Yahweh tells her to return to her mistress Sarai and submit to her, for Hagar's descendants through Ishmael will be so numerous "that they cannot be numbered for multitude" (16:10). In the second instance, the angel shows Hagar water in the wilderness and informs her once again that God will make Ishmael into "a great nation" (21:18).

Ishmael is included in the covenant of circumcision that God establishes with his father Abraham (17:25–26). And the names of his twelve sons are listed in the order of their birth (25:13–15). Jewish tradition suggests that Abraham's wife Keturah is in fact Hagar, which would make her five sons brothers of Ishmael (25:1–2). Nonetheless, the biblical text is clear that Isaac is Abraham's primary heir and his other son is sent away.

Within the concentric structure of Genesis as a whole, the disturbing story of the *Akedah* (the binding of Isaac) in Genesis 22 functions as both the concluding episode in the Abraham narrative cycle and as a center within the center of the book of Genesis. The story of Isaac may also be outlined in a menorah pattern with the *Akedah* at its center, as follows:

Isaac the Promised Son of God's Covenant — Genesis 18–35

A Birth of Isaac, as promised by "angels"	18:1–15; 21:1–7
B Abraham's two sons—story of Isaac and Ishmael	21:8–21
C Abraham and Abimelech—Abraham's sojourn in Philistia	21:22–34
X The *Akedah*—binding of Isaac (testing of Abraham)	22:1–19
C´ Isaac and Abimelech—Isaac's sojourn with the Philistines	26:1–33
B´ Isaac's two sons—story of Jacob and Esau	26:34–35:27
A´ Death of Isaac at 180 years of age	35:28–29

The specific boundaries in this concentric structural design are difficult to delineate because of the presence of material that belongs to other narrative structures. These blocks of material include the story of Abraham and Sarah (Gen 18:16–20:34), the genealogy of Nahor (Gen 22:20–24), the concluding stories about Abraham and Sarah after the *Akedah* (Gen 23:1–25:11), a genealogy of Ishmael (25:12–18), and an introduction to the rivalry between Jacob and Esau (Gen 25:19–27).

In the story of the *Akedah*, Abraham is commanded by God to sacrifice his "only son" Isaac (Gen 22:2) as a burnt offering on Mount Moriah, which is subsequently identified with the Temple Mount in Jerusalem. This story has profound ties to the sacrificial death of another "only (begotten) son" on Golgotha ("place of the skull"), outside the city walls in ancient Jerusalem many centuries later, as a number of the early Church Fathers saw so clearly. In patristic theology, Isaac is presented as an example of the perfect sacrifice that foreshadows the crucified Messiah Yeshua (Jesus Christ).

3. The Matriarchs in the Book of Genesis

Abraham, Isaac and Jacob are traditionally known as the Patriarchs and their wives Sarah, Rebekah and Rachel are sometimes called "Matriarchs." Sarah is the mother of Isaac, Rebekah the mother of Jacob and Esau, and Rachel the mother of Joseph and Benjamin. Jacob's secondary wife Leah must be added to the list, for she is the mother of six of the twelve sons/tribes of Israel, including Judah, and the mother of Dinah as well. The two slaves of Leah and Rachel, Bilhah and Zilpah, are the mothers of the other four sons/tribes of Israel (Dan & Naphtali and Gad & Asher); and thus must be added to the list of "Matriarchs" in Genesis. The addition of Hagar, mother of Ishmael, to this list raises the question of Asenath, wife of Joseph, who should be added to the list as well, as the following menorah pattern suggests:

The Matriarchs of Genesis in a Menorah Pattern
A   Hagar—Egyptian slave and mother of Ishmael (father of twelve Arab "princes")
B   Sarah—mother of Isaac (promised son of blessing)
C   Rebekah—mother of Jacob/Israel and Esau/Edom
X   **Leah—mother of Reuben, Simeon, Levi, Judah, Issachar, Zebulun and Dinah**
C´   Bilhah (mother of Dan and Naphtali) and Zilpah (mother of Gad and Asher)
B´   Rachel—mother of Joseph and Benjamin
A´ Asenath—Egyptian wife of Joseph and mother of Ephraim and Manasseh

The fertile Egyptian wives Hagar and Asenath, form an envelope around the theme of barrenness, which includes Sarah, Rebekah and Rachel. That theme ends with the death of Rachel in childbirth at the birth of Benjamin near Bethlehem. The framework in this concentric narrative structure moves from Hagar to Leah to Asenath, in which fertility is a dominant motif. In sharp contrast, Sarah and Rachel present the theme of barrenness in that each takes matters into her own hands to have a "legal child" through her slave, Hagar and Bilhah.

Within Jewish tradition, Dinah is added to the list of "Matriarchs" as well, for she is Job's second wife—after his ordeal—who bore him seven sons and three daughters (a reflection in reverse of the three Patriarchs and their seven women—the mothers of the fathers, as it were, in those first three generations). The Mishna presents Job as a "crypto-patriarch," the son-in-law of Jacob, through his marriage to Dinah, and a brother-in-law of the twelve sons/tribes of Israel. The Matriarch Hagar has the honor of starting the whole narrative sequence in the birth of Ishmael, who in turn is the father of twelve "princes" among the Arab descendants of Abraham, the "father of a multitude of nations" (Gen 17:5).

Concept Check #3

What is Hagar's role within the narrative structure of the book of Genesis?

Check your answer at the back of this book.

D. Genesis 1–11 and the Book of Jonah From Torah to Latter Prophets

Genesis 1–11 functions as an introduction to the Bible and knowledge of its content is presupposed in narratives elsewhere in the Tanakh. Moreover, some stories are actually shaped by the structure and vocabulary of these chapters. As we will see in the next chapter of this book, the story of Moses' birth in Exodus 1–2 is shaped by the story of Noah in Genesis 6–9. In particular, the account of the salvation of the infant Moses from the waters of chaos and death by means of an "ark" (*tebah*) is dependent on the description of Noah's ark (*tebah*) in the Great Flood, as James Ackerman has demonstrate.[1] Genesis 6–9 and Exodus 2 are the only two places in the Bible where the word "ark" (*tebah*) appears. Anyone who heard the story of Exodus 2 recited in ancient Israel could not help but think of the familiar story of Noah and the flood, and perhaps vice versa; for the allusion is intentional.

The story of Jonah presents an instructive example of how Genesis 1–11 is used to shape a narrative elsewhere in the Tanakh. The narrative progression in the book of Jonah is the reverse of what is found in Genesis 1–11, as the following chart suggests:[2]

Jonah		Genesis 1–11	
A Fleeing from Tarshish		Dispersion	
not going to Mesopotamia		coming out of Mesopotamia	
despite God's will	1:1–3	according to God's will	11:1–32
Nineveh	1:2	Babel / Shin'ar	11:1, 9
Jonah: "I am a Hebrew"	1:9	Abram, the Hebrew	14:13
B Flood, *nahar*	1:4–15	Flood, *mabul*	chs. 6–9
ship of tribulation	1:5	ship of salvation	chs. 6–9
Jonah = dove		dove (released from the ark)	8:10–12
waves pass over Jonah	2:4	wind passes over the earth	8:1
tehom ("deep") surrounds	2:6	*tehom* bursts forth	7:11
bottoms of mountains	2:7	tops of mountains	8:5
Jonah remembers Yahweh	2:8	God remembers Noah	8:1
in 40 days	3:4	end of 40 days	8:6

---

1   J. S. Ackerman, "The Literary Context of the Moses Birth Story," in *Literary Interpretations of Biblical Narratives*, eds. E. Gros Louis, et al (Nashville: Abingdon Press, 1974), pp. 74-119.

2   Adopted from E. Hesse and I. Kikawada, "Jonah and Genesis 11-1," *Annual of the Japanese Biblical Institute* 10 (184), pp. 3-19; see D. L. Christensen, "Jonah and the Sabbath Rest in the Pentateuch," in *Biblische Theologie und gesellschaftlicher Wandel: Für Norbert Lohfink SJ*, eds. G. Braulik, et al (Herder, 1993), pp. 48-60.

C Jonah's anger and *tob* ("good")		Cain's anger and *tob* ("good")	
in causative stem	4:4	in causative stem	4:7, 9
driven out before God	2:5	driven out of God's presence	4:14
hebel = (vain) idols	2:9	Abel = *hebel*	4:2
Jonah wants to die	4:4	Cain wants to live	4:13–14
Jonah "dwells" east of city	4:5	Cain "dwells" east of Eden	4:16
D *Qiqayon* (plant) and Worm	4:6–7	Tree and Snake	2:5–3:24
Protection from evil	4:6	cause for evil	3:22
glad because of plant's shade	4:6	tree is delightful	3:6
worm causes plant to wither	4:7	snake entices to eat of tree	3:4–5
plant taken away = test	4:7	tree given = test	3:4–5
Jonah wants to die because of plant	4:9	eat of fruit and surely die	2:17
E God cares for both humans & beasts	4:11	God creates beasts and humans	1:1–2:3
seven narrative days (implied)	ending	seven days of creation	ch. 1

Through the years, numerous students of the Bible have observed that the first six days of creation in Genesis 1 are arranged in parallel 3-day "panels" as follows:

Panel One	Panel Two
Day 1 Light (1:3–5)	Day 4 Lights: sun, moon and stars (1:14–19)
Day 2 Firmament (1:6–8	Day 5 Inhabitants (1:20–23)
Sky	Fish
Seas	Birds
Day 3 Dry Land (1:9–10)	Day 6 Land animals (1:24–26)
Vegetation (1:11–13)	Human beings (1:27–31)

The physical domains of the universe and immovable objects on earth are created in the first three days. In the second three days, the movable things are created for each of the days in the first "panel" of three days. The chiastic reversal of the products of the middle days adds to the symmetry, as Mark Thronveit has noted.[3]

A close look at the seven days of creation reflected in the book of Jonah reveals a three-day structure in each half of the book, with a "Sabbath" allocated to the implied ending of the story, which parallels the structure of the creation account in Genesis 1. Moreover, the motif of three days and three night in the belly of the "Great Fish" in Jonah 1–2 ultimately becomes on the lips of Yeshua the Messiah (Jesus Christ) the "sign of Jonah" in Matt 12:39–40.

Jonah's sojourn inside the "Great Fish" constitutes the first of two 3-day cycles in the book of Jonah. The journey of three days in the second half of the book is less clear such that it goes unnoticed in the commentaries. In Jonah 3:3, the city of Nineveh is described as a "great city" *to God*, namely *a journey of three days*. On the first day of Jonah's journey to Nineveh ("the house of the fish"), Jonah uttered his prophetic message of merely five words in the Hebrew text, which may be rendered: "There remain but forty days and Nineveh

---

3   M. A. Thronveit, "Are the Events in the Genesis Creation Account Set Forth in Chronological Order?" in *The Genesis Debate: Persistent Questions about Creation and the Flood*, ed. R. Youngblood (New York: Thomas Nelson, 1986), p. 46.

shall be *overturned*." To Jonah this meant that Nineveh would suffer the fate of Sodom and Gomorrah in Gen 19:25, when God "overthrew" those cities. It should be noted, however, that elsewhere in the Tanakh (Hebrew Bible) the primary meaning of the word translated "overturned" in Jonah 3:4 is "to turn (something over)" or "to change." The word can even mean, "to be given another heart" in the sense of conversion (cf. 1 Sam 10:9, where God "changes" Saul's heart). And has there ever been a description of a greater conversion of a wicked city than the narrative of Jonah 3:5–9? This was an example of "power evangelism" greater than anything recorded in the Acts of the Apostles. The city of Nineveh was indeed "overturned." Its *conversion* was so impressive that God himself was subsequently *converted* as well—that is, God "repented from the evil which he said he would do to them; and he did not do it" (Jonah 3:10). In other words, the prophetic words of the prophet were fulfilled exactly as God intended. The only problem is that the prophet did not understand the meaning of his own prophetic words. They meant one thing to him, and precisely the opposite to the God who gave him those very words.

The first time "dry land" appears in the Tanakh is on the third day of creation, when God gathered the waters into one place and the *dry land* appeared (1:9)—and "God called the *dry land* Earth, and the waters that were gathered together he called Seas" (1:10, RSV). At the end of the book of Jonah, the reluctant prophet has the opportunity to take his place together with God on another "third day" of creation; the second of two such "third days" in that story—which, thus, corresponds to the climactic sixth day in Genesis 1. In the first such instance, God restores the reluctant prophet from the belly of the "Great Fish" and launches him once again on his calling in the completion of God's task of creation among the nations. On the second of these "third days" of creation, Jonah is given the opportunity to restore himself to a proper understanding of his calling within the process of God's greater work of creation (cf. Gen 1:28). If Jonah "rises" to the occasion, he will experience God's "Sabbath rest," which is intended for all *animals* and *human beings* created on the sixth day of creation in Gen 1:24–28 (to which compare the repeated phrase *human beings and animals* in Jonah 3:7–8).

Jewish legend adds substance to this interpretation of the book of Jonah; for, according to tradition, the fish intended to harbor Jonah was made at the creation of the world.[4] Though it is not explicitly stated, it is conceivable that the "Great Fish," like the ram of the *Akedah* ("binding" of Isaac) in Genesis 22, was among those special acts of creation in the twilight of the first Sabbath eve. And this is precisely where the book of Jonah ends symbolically.

In short, God's great act of creation is not yet complete. It is God who poses the disturbing question in the concluding verse of the book of Jonah (4:11): "Should I not have compassion on Nineveh, that great city in which there are more than 120,000 human beings . . . and also many cattle?" The implied answer to this question is a resounding "Yes!" And when Jonah shares that same compassion for all "human beings"—and the animals as well—he will prove to be instrumental in the completion of creation itself, which is climaxed in a great Sabbath rest. In that day, Jonah and God will together enjoy

---

4   L. Ginzberg, *The Legends of the Jews*, vol. 4 (Philadelphia: Jewish Publication Society, 1954), p. 249.

conversation in the "Garden of Eden," as suggested in the schematic diagram above of the seven days of creation, as reflected in the book of Jonah.

> ### Concept Check #4
>
> What does the structural relationship between Genesis 1–11 and Jonah, as presented here, suggest about the composition of Genesis and Jonah as books in the Bible?
>
> Check your answer at the back of this book.

E. Genesis within the Bible as a Whole

The story of Israel as a national entity begins with the birth of Moses in Exodus 1 and ends with the death of Moses and the transition in leadership to his successor Joshua in Deuteronomy 34. At the same time, this "Moses Story" takes place within a larger structural frame, which extends from creation to the eschaton. Within this narrative framework we find the nesting of parallel features, which may be outlined in an elaborate seven-part series of nested menorah patterns ("wheels within wheels"):

The Tanakh in a Menorah Pattern   *Torah / Prophets / Writings*

A   Primeval History   Genesis 1–11
B   Patriarchs: Abraham, Isaac and Jacob   Genesis 12–36
C   Joseph and his eleven brothers (esp. Judah)   Genesis 37–50
X   **Journey to the Promised Land**   **Exodus—Deuteronomy**
C´   Former Prophets   Joshua, Judges, 1–2 Samuel and 1–2 Kings
B´   Latter Prophets   Isaiah, Jeremiah, Ezekiel and The Twelve
A´ Writings of the Tanakh   Hagiographa (4), Daniel and Chronicler's History (4)

2ⁿᵈ Level Menorah: Journey to the Promised Land   *Exodus–Deuteronomy*

A   Birth of Moses—God's chosen leader for the people of Israel   Exod 1:1–22
B   Moses is called to leadership—the Exodus   2:1–14:31
C   *Song of Moses* at crossing of *Yam Suf* (Sea of Reeds)   15:1–21
X   **From the Exodus to the Eisodus**   Exod 15:22–Deut 31:29
C´   *Song of Moses* in the plains of Moab   Deut 32:52
B´   Blessing of Moses—anticipating the Eisodus   33:1–29
A´ Death of Moses and transition of leadership to Joshua   34:1–12

3ʳᵈ Level Menorah: From the Exodus to the Eisodus   *Exod 15:22–Deut 31:29*

A   Journey from *Yam Suf* (Sea of Reeds) to Mount Sinai   Exod 15:22–19:25
B   Covenant Code—including the Ten Commandments   20:1–23:33
C   Revelation at Sinai: covenant with Israel made and broken   24:1–33:22
X   **Yahweh's tabernacling presence with his people**   Exod 34–Deut 5
C´   Revelation at Sinai: preparation for covenant renewal   Deut 6:1–11:32
B´   Deuteronomic Code—built on the Ten Commandments   12:1–26:19
A´ Journey from Moab across the Jordan River (anticipated)   27:1–31:30

4th *Level: Yahweh's Tabernacling Presence with His People*   *Exodus 34–Deut 5*

A	Second giving of the Ten Commandments	Exodus 34
B	At Mount Sinai, "Moses finished the work" (40:33)	Exod 35:1–40:33
C	The cloud and glory—God's tabernacling presence	Exod 40:34–Lev 27
X	**Forty Years waiting to enter the Promised Land**	Numbers 1–36
C´	The Eisodus into Transjordan under Moses	Deut 1:1–3:22
B´	In the plains of Moab, Moses finished his work	Deut 3:23–4:49
A´	Theophany and covenant at Horeb—the Ten Commandments	Deuteronomy 5

5th *Level: Forty Years Waiting to Enter the Promised Land*   *Numbers 1–36*

A	Israel prepares to enter the Promised Land	1:1–10:36
B	Journey from Mount Sinai to Kadesh in the wilderness of Paran	11:1–35
C	Political rebellion on the part of Miriam and Aaron	12:1–16
X	**Rebellion in the Wilderness**	13:1–20:21
C´	Death of Aaron at Mount Hor (Miriam died at Kadesh [20:1])	20:22–29
B´	Journey from Kadesh to the plains of Moab	21:1–25:18
A´	Israel prepares to enter the Promised Land	26:1–36:13

6th *Level Menorah: Rebellion in the Wilderness*   *Num 13:1–20:21*

A	Disaster at Kadesh—rebellion of the spies	13:1–14:45
B	Laws on cultic matters—stoning narrative for Sabbath violation	15:1–41
C	Rebellion: Korah, Dathan and Abiram swallowed by the earth	16:1–33
X	**Way of atonement is provided through Aaron**	16:34–17:13
C´	Levites are given the tithe as their tribal allotment	18:1–32
B´	Laws on matters of defilement—the red heifer	19:1–22
A´	Waters of Meribah and the "rebellion" of Moses	20:1–21

7th *Level: Way of Atonement is Provided through Aaron*   *Num 16:34–17:13*

A	All Israel fled saying, "The earth will swallow us too!"	16:34–35
B	Making of the bronze covering for the altar from rebels' censers	16:36–40
C	Rebellion of the congregation—God decides to "consume them"	16:41–45
X	**Moses commands Aaron to make atonement for the people**	16:46
C´	Aaron takes incense in a censer and stays the plague	16:47–50
B´	Test of the rods—Aaron's rod blooms to end the murmuring	17:1–12
A´	The Israelites are afraid: "Are we all to perish?"	17:13

The story of Moses as founder of the religion of ancient Israel is the structural center of a menorah pattern that embraces the whole of the Tanakh. The stories in the Primeval History (Genesis 1–11), from Adam to Abram, are set over against the Writings of the Tanakh. And the story of the Fathers (Abraham, Isaac, Jacob, and his twelve sons) is set over against the Latter Prophets (Isaiah, Jeremiah, Ezekiel, and the Book of the Twelve [lesser prophets]). The story of Joseph and his brothers, with particular interest in Judah in Genesis 37–50, anticipates the story of the Former Prophets (Joshua through 2 Kings). Joseph (through his sons Ephraim and Manasseh) and Judah dominate the story of the nation of Israel in the Promised Land in the Former Prophets, as their eponymous ancestors do in the narrative of Genesis. And in the structural center of the Tanakh as a whole we find the epic story of Israel's journey home to the land of Canaan, from slavery in the land of Egypt—i.e., the "Moses Story." As we will see, that story is also called the "wars of Yahweh."

Concept Check #5

What is the central story in the book of Genesis?
Check your answer at the back of this book.

The Pentateuchal Structure of the Book of Genesis

[Four Wheels of the Same Likeness and a Wheel within the Four Wheels]

A	*The Primeval History—from Adam to Abram*	*Genesis 1–11*
a	Creation of Adam and Eve to the birth of Seth	1:1–4:26
b	Generations of Adam and his three sons	5:1–32
x	Noah and the Great Flood—a new creation (9:1; cf. 1:28)	6:1–9:29
b´	Generations of Noah and his three sons	10:1–32
a´	Dispersion of the descendants of Shem—to Abram and Sarai	11:1–32

B	*Abraham and His Familiy—Esau Sells His Birthright*	*Gen 12:1–25:18*
a	Abram and Sarai—foreshadowing the Exodus from Egypt	12:1–20
b	Abram and the promise of land	13:1–14:24
x	God's covenant with Abram/Abraham and Ishmael	15:1–17:27
b´	Abraham and the promise of progeny through Isaac	18:1–22:24
a´	Isaac and Rebekah—hope for the future	23:1–25:18

X	*Isaac Blesses Jacob and Esau*	*Gen 25:19–28:5*
a	Jacob and Esau—Isaac seeks refuge in Philistia (Gerar)	25:19–26:33
b	Esau's Hittite wives	26:34–35
x	Isaac blesses Jacob	27:1–29
b´	Esau's lesser blessing	27:30–40
a´	Jacob and Esau—Jacob seeks refuge in Padan-aram	27:41–28:5

B´	*Jacob and His Family—Esau's Descendants (Edom)*	*Gen 28:6–36:43*
a	Esau marries Mahalath, the daughter of Ishmael	28:6–9
b	Jacob's flight to Bethel and to Haran where he lives for 20 years	28:10–30:24
x	Birth of Joseph ["May Yahweh add another (son)!"	30:25–26
b´	Jacob's return from Haran to Bethel—death of Rachel and Isaac	30:27–35:27
a´	Esau's descendants—the clans and kings of Edom	36:1–42

A´	*Special History Foreshadowed—Israel's Twelve Sons/Tribes*	*Genesis 37–50*
a	Joseph and his dreams	37:1–36
b	Judah and Tamar	38:1–30
x	Joseph in Egypt—his rise to power by interpreting dreams	39:1–44:17
b´	Judah's speech: "(Keep me) in place of the boy (Benjamin)"	44:18–34
a´	Fulfillment of Joseph's dreams—Jacob's family in Egypt	45:1–50:26

Study Questions

These study questions are optional and are designed for the student who wishes to go beyond what is required. *Do not send them to the Center for evaluation.*

1. In the light of the menorah patterns presented in this chapter, what is the central message of the book of Genesis?

2. What do you feel are the four or five most important events in Genesis 1–11? Why?

3. What do you think are the three or four events in Abraham's life that helped most to develop his character?

4. What three events do you think contributed more than any others to Jacob's spiritual growth?

5. Prepare a title or a phrase that would best characterize the life of Joseph. Justify your answer.

6. In light of the narrative structures presented in this chapter, who is the anticipated "son of God" in terms of the covenant of circumcision?

7. Discuss the importance of reading Genesis 1–11 as an introduction to the Bible as a whole.

8. Select the "Matriarch" that appeals most to you and justify your choice.

9. Discuss the concept of Job as a "crypto-patriarch."

The Book of Exodus

Contents

A. Exodus and the Wars of Yahweh
B. Moses as Leader in Ancient Israel
C. Reading the Book of Exodus from the Center
D. The Tabernacle in the Religion of Israel
E. Passover within the Canonical Process

Objectives

When this chapter is completed, the student should be able to:

♦ Summarize the major events in the deliverance of Israel from Egypt
♦ Discuss the basic concept of the Mosaic covenant
♦ Describe the Tabernacle and its contents
♦ Identify two different "centers" in the book of Exodus
♦ Explain the significance of the Festival of Passover in the Bible
♦ Explain the relationship between the books of Exodus and Deuteronomy

A. Exodus and the Wars of Yahweh

In Jewish tradition, the name of the second book of the Torah is שמות (pronounced *Shemot*), shortened from the opening two words in the Hebrew text *ve'elleh shemot*, "These are the names." The key concepts in the book are redemption and revelation. God delivers his people from slavery in Egypt and reveals his will to them through Moses on Mount Sinai. God continues to deal with his chosen people—even though they are not faithful to the terms of the covenant he establishes with them.

The story begins with the birth of Moses and ends with the completion of the Tabernacle, which houses the glory of Yahweh. The book of Exodus may be outlined in a nested menorah pattern, as follows:

The Book of Exodus in a Menorah Pattern   *Exodus 1–40*

A   God delivers the people from Egypt—pillars of cloud and fire   1:1–15:19
B   Journey to Sinai with God's provision in the wilderness   15:20–17:16
C   Jethro's visit—Moses organizes the judicial leadership   18:1–27
X   **Three-fold theophany on Sinai—God reveals himself**   19:1–24:14
C´   Moses spends forty days on the mountain with God   24:15–18
B´   The building of the Tabernacle at Mount Sinai   25:1–40:33
A´ Yahweh's glory fills the Tabernacle—the cloud and the fire   40:34–38

2nd Level Menorah: Three-Fold Theophany on Mount Sinai   *Exod 19:1–24:14*

A   God's invitation for Israel to be "a kingdom of priests"   19:1–6
B   Theophany: Moses brings the people out to meet God   19:7–25
C   Giving of the Ten Commandments (orally)   20:1–17
X   **Theophany: Moses meets God in thick darkness**   20:18–21
C´   Book of the Covenant—oldest legislation in the Bible   20:22–23:33
B´   Theophany: Moses brings the leadership to "see" God   24:1–11
A´ Invitation for Moses to receive the gift of the stone tablets   24:12–14

The outermost frame in this structure focuses on the image of the numinous cloud and fire, in which Yahweh guides the people of Israel in their epic journey from slavery in Egypt to the Promised Land. After Pharaoh finally lets the people go, God leads them through the wilderness with a pillar of cloud by day and a pillar of fire by night (Exod 13:21–22). Exodus concludes with the cloud covering the Meeting Tent and the glory of Yahweh filling the Tabernacle that Moses erects at Mount Sinai (Exod 40:34–38). The cloud and the glory are present when Moses ascends the mountain in the theophany at the center of the book (24:13–18). Moses spends forty days and forty nights in the cloud and "the appearance of the glory of Yahweh is like a devouring fire on the top of the mountain in the sight of the people of Israel" (24:17, RSV).

The focus of attention here is on a three-fold theophany at Mount Sinai. God reveals himself to Moses "in thick darkness" (20:21)—along with the Ten Commandments (20:1–17) and the "Book of the Covenant" (20:22–24:18), which are given to Moses orally. In the second frame, Moses leads the people of Israel on their journey from *Yam Suf* (Sea of Reeds) to Mount Sinai (15:22–18:27). On this journey God supplies them with food and water in the wilderness (16:1–17:7). The second frame concludes with a detailed account of the work that God instructs Moses to do at Mount Sinai—the building of the Tabernacle (25:1–40:33).

Another way of looking at the structure of Exodus as a whole is to divide the book in half—into two "wheels of the same likeness," as follows:

1st Half: From Egypt to Mount Sinai—Theophany   *Exod 1:1–24:12*

A   Birth, naming and call of Moses   1:1–3:12
B   Theophany at the burning bush—Yahweh reveals his name   3:13–15
C   Contest with Pharaoh—the ten plagues and Passover   5:1–13:22
X   **Crossing of the Sea and the Song of Moses**   14:1–15:21
C´   Crises in the wilderness and war with Amalek   15:22–18:27
B´   Theophany—Yahweh reveals laws on Mount Sinai   19:1–23:33
A´ Moses on the mountain with Yahweh   24:1–12

2nd Half: At Mount Sinai—Theophany and Tabernacle — Exod 24:13–40:38

A	Moses and Joshua on the mountain of God—the cloud and glory	24:13–18
B	Tabernacle planned	25:1–31:18
C	Covenant broken—Golden Calf incident	32:1–33:6
X	**Moses and Joshua in the Meeting Tent—cloud and glory**	33:7–23
C´	Covenant renewed—with two new tablets of stone	34:1–35
B´	Tabernacle built	35:1–40:33
A´	Yahweh's tabernacling presence—the cloud and glory	40:34–38

Unlike the book of Genesis, the boundary between the two major sections of Exodus does not fall precisely on the boundary of one of the weekly portions (Parashoth) in the annual cycle of readings from the Torah. The concluding verses of Parashah 18 (Exod 24:13–18), which is in the first half of the book, appear to be an essential part of the framework in the menorah pattern for the second half. Here we find specific mention of *the cloud* and *the glory of Yahweh*, which is reiterated in 33:7–23, at the center, and again in the concluding note in 40:34–38.

The center of the first half of Exodus is the pivotal event of the crossing of *Yam Suf* (Sea of Reeds) and the Song of Moses, which Moses taught the people at that momentous occasion in the formation of Israel as a nation (14:1–15:21). The outermost frame opens with the account of the birth, naming, and call of Moses (1:1–3:12). It continues with the presentation of Moses, Aaron, Nadab, Abihu, and seventy of the elders of Israel who "saw the God of Israel . . . they beheld God, and ate and drank" on Mount Sinai (24:10–11). The second frame in this structure moves from the theophany at the burning bush, when Yahweh reveals his name to Moses (3:13–15), to the theophany at Mount Sinai (Exodus 19–23), where God reveals the stipulations of his covenant agreement in the form of specific laws. The innermost frame opens with a lengthy account of the contest with Pharaoh in the series of ten plagues (Exodus 5–13), which reach their climax in the "passing over" of the angel of death. It continues with the story of crises in the wilderness on route to Mount Sinai, which reach their climax in the war against Amalek (17:8–16).

The menorah pattern of the second half of Exodus reveals two themes that tie the section together as a whole. In the first place, the cloud and the glory appear in all three parts of the structural framework (A, X, A´). In the second, Joshua is present with Moses at the beginning (24:13) and in the middle (33:11). The importance of this latter observation is shown in the following menorah pattern, which embraces the whole of the Hexateuch (Genesis through Joshua):

Joshua at the Structural Center of the Hexateuch — Genesis–Joshua

A	From Creation to the breaking of the covenant at Mount Sinai	Genesis 1–Exodus 32
B	Yahweh speaks: I will not go with this "stiff-necked people"	Exod 33:1–6
C	Moses experiences Yahweh's presence in the Meeting Tent	33:7–11a
X	**Joshua does not depart from the Meeting Tent**	33:11b
C´	Moses will experience Yahweh's presence in the future	33:12–16
B´	Yahweh speaks: I will show you a glimpse of my glory	33:17–23
A´	Covenant renewal—from Mount Sinai to Shechem	Exodus 34–Joshua 24

The reference to Joshua here functions as a "riddle in the middle," in that the reason is not immediately evident. It is only when the reader looks at the larger context of the Hexateuch (Genesis through Joshua) as a whole, that the puzzle is solved. The note concerning Joshua in the Meeting Tent serves as an envelope with both the end of the book of Deuteronomy (chaps. 31 and 34) and the book of Joshua as a whole. Joshua begins his role of leadership in Exod 17:8–16, as a military general in the war against Amalek—the traditional "enemy of the Jews." But in this war, Moses is still the commander-in-chief. "Whenever Moses held up his hand, Israel prevailed; and whenever he lowered his hand, Amalek prevailed" (17:11).

The wars of Yahweh are in two parts—the Exodus from Egypt under Moses and the Eisodus (Entry) into the Promised Land under Joshua. The Eisodus in turn is also in two parts—the trek from the crossing of *Yam Suf* (Sea of Reeds; i.e., the defeat of Pharaoh's armies in the Exodus from Egypt) to the battle camp at Shittim, near Mount Nebo, when Joshua assumes the role of commander-in-chief at the death of Moses. The first phase of the Eisodus reaches its culmination with the conquest of the two Amorite kings, Sihon and Og, in Transjordan. The second phase begins with the crossing of the Jordan River into Cisjordan, after Moses' death on Mount Nebo.

Joshua appears as a military leader under Moses' command in the war against the Amalekites, which takes place before the people of Israel have reached Mount Sinai to establish their covenant with Yahweh. Joshua serves under Moses throughout the whole of the first phase of the Eisodus, and he succeeds Moses as commander-in-chief for the second phase. The fact that he "did not depart from the tent" (Exod 33:11) explains Joshua's success as a leader, for Joshua is engaged in fighting the wars of Yahweh. When a leader of God's people chooses to depart from the tent of "Yahweh's presence," the undoing of God's blessing has already begun. The nature of this unfortunate process is explored in depth in the covenant curses of the book of Deuteronomy.

Concept Check #6

Would it be better to use the word "Tetrateuch" to describe the books of Exodus through Deuteronomy rather than Genesis through Numbers? Why or why not?

Check your answer at the back of this book.

B. Moses as Leader in Israel

In his study of Moses as a political leader, Aaron Wildavsky makes an invaluable contribution to the field of biblical studies, as well as to his own specialty, political science.[1] Wildavsky uses the Torah is a source for teaching the theory of leadership as a function

---

1   Aaron Wildavsky, *The Nursing Father: Moses as a Political Leader* (University of Alabama Press, 1984).

of political regime. At the same time, he shows that viewing the Torah as a teaching about leadership enhances its interpretation. His study illustrates the need for fluency in the use of the biblical story in order to apply that content to an important issue—the nature of leadership.

As Wildavsky notes (*The Nursing Father*, p. 201), Moses exemplifies leadership in at least eight areas. He is:

1. *Founder* of a nation
2. *Revolutionary*—transforming three different political regimes
3. *Lawgiver* whose laws have lasted thousands of years
4. *Administrator* of two political regimes
5. *Storyteller* whose words have become deeds
6. *Teacher* of a way of life that still lives
7. *Student* who exemplifies learning how to learn
8. *Politician* balancing conflicting values within himself and among his people

As the Torah itself insists, there is none with which to compare Moses—"there has not arisen a prophet like Moses . . . none like him . . . for all the mighty power and all the great and terrible deeds which Moses wrought in the sight of all Israel" (Deut 34: 10–12). The Mosaic experience has much to teach us about leadership, but not in the sense of providing us with a specific example to follow.

When Moses transforms the polity of ancient Israel from a regime of equity into one of hierarchy on that long journey to the Promised Land, we find an inherent tension in the demands of leadership that ultimately produces the biblical principle we call the "Samuel Compromise." It is not the choice between these two regimes we are seeking; it is a balance between them. It takes a balance of power to live within the tension of these two regimes. In the history of ancient Israel this is achieved by Samuel, the last of the judges, with the institution of two separate offices—that of prophet and king. Moses as a political leader combines these two roles in one person.

The story of Deborah and Barak in Judges 4–5 foreshadows the new paradigm of leadership in Israel. After Moses, the paradigm of the prophet (*nabi'*) in ancient Israel, Deborah is the first political figure to emerge with that title (Judg 4:4). Though Barak never becomes a "king" as such, his role in the story models the role required of the king who lives according to the Torah. When Barak is asked to lead the army of Israel in battle against the Canaanites, he says to Deborah, "If you will go with me, I will go; but if you will not go with me, I will not go" (Judg 4:8). The "good king" within the Former Prophets is the one who recognizes the authority of the prophet whom God raises up at that moment in Israel's history. In short, two very different types of leaders are needed, at the same time, within the ongoing community of faith in the Bible—the prophet and the king. It is almost impossible to combine these two roles in a single person.

Leadership in ancient Israel requires a splitting apart of the contradictory roles personified in Moses as he makes the transition from the regime of equity to that of hierarchy. The prophet (*nabi'*) is the one who rules according to the principle of the regime Wildavsky calls equity. The prophet is the charismatic leader whose power is unlimited but discontinuous—within a given situation, such as the war between Israel and the

Canaanites in the story of Deborah and Barak. In the so-called Samuel Compromise, the corresponding role of "king" appears first in the Hebrew word *nagid* (permanent war-lord), where the leader's role is limited, continuous, and autocratic. It is only when a balance of power is achieved between the *nabi'* and the *nagid* as leaders that the people enjoy the fullness of God's blessing. Moses combines these two roles, along with other roles as well. In so doing, Moses foreshadows both types of leader; and the Torah becomes a handbook of leadership, which is summarized in the law of the king (Deut 17:14–20) and the law of the prophets (Deut 18:9–22).

Concept Check #7

Do you see any parallels between the story of the life of Moses, as it is told here, and the story of God's chosen people that is about to unfold in the biblical account?

Check your answer at the back of this book.

C. Reading the Book of Exodus from the Center

1. The Eleven Parashoth in the Book of Exodus

Study of the eleven Parashoth (weekly portions in the annual cycle of readings from the Torah in Judaism) suggests that the scribes of antiquity divided Exodus into four major divisions, each of which may be outlined in a menorah pattern—or "four wheels of the same likeness":

A	Exodus from Egypt—institution of Passover	Exodus 1–17	Parashoth 13–16
B	Theophany and covenant at Mount Sinai	Exodus 18–24	Parashoth 17–18
B´	Covenant broken and renewed at Mount Sinai	Exodus 25–34	Parashoth 19–21
A´	Establishing Israel's worship in the Tabernacle	Exodus 35–40	Parashoth 22–23

The lengthy detailed description of the plans for the Tabernacle in Exodus 25–31, and the parallel account of its construction in 35:1–38:20, make it difficult for most readers to see the chiastic nature of the narrative itself. In the two central sections of Exodus, we find parallel theophanies—one detailed (Exodus 19–24) and the other relatively brief (Exodus 33). The latter is buried between these extended presentations of the plans for and subsequent construction of the Tabernacle.

   The focus of attention in the first major section (Exodus 1–17) is on the establishment of the Festival of Passover and Unleavened Bread (Exodus 12), which subsequently becomes the first and most important of three pilgrimage festivals in ancient Israel. Laws concerning the three annual festivals are found in Exod 34:18–24. Moreover, the Tabernacle itself becomes the symbol of Yahweh's abiding presence in the midst of his people—and the destination of the three annual pilgrimages to the central sanctuary.

a. Exodus from Egypt—Institution of Passover (Exodus 1–17)

The first "wheel," with its presentation of the Exodus from Egypt and the institution of Passover, may be outlined in a menorah pattern:

Parashoth 13–16: Exodus from Egypt—Institution of Passover	*Exodus 1–17*
A Israel's situation in Egypt and Pharaoh's decree of death	1:1–22
B The naming of Moses and his call to deliver Israel from Egypt	2:1–4:31
C Contest with Pharaoh—climaxed with death of the first-born	5:1–11:10
X **Passover and Unleavened Bread—departure from Egypt**	12:1–50
C´ Consecration of the first-born	13:1–16
B´ Israel's deliverance—the crossing of the sea	13:17–15:19
A´ Crises in the wilderness and war with Amalek	15:20–17:16

The "wars of Yahweh" begin with the defeat of Pharoah and his armies in the Exodus from Egypt. This story opens with an account of Pharaoh's decree, that "Every son that is born to the Hebrews you shall cast into the Nile" (1:22). This opening episode in this epic story of deliverance is set over against the account of Israel's subsequent experience in the wilderness of Sin, with its climax in the war against Amalek (17:8–16). This marks the beginning of another phase in the wars of Yahweh, which culminates in the conquest of the land of Canaan under Joshua—who commanded the forces of Israel against the Amalekites at the outset in the journey to the Promised Land (17:10).

The name Moses, which Pharaoh's daughter gives the infant when she draws him out of the water (Exodus 2:10), actually means "one who draws (the people) through (the waters)." In short, the participle is active in nature and not passive. As such, the name Moses (*Mosheh*) foreshadows his mission, which is presented in the other half of the second frame in this menorah pattern (13:17–15:21). The contest between Moses and Pharaoh is presented in a series of ten plagues, which reach their climax in the death of the first-born in Egypt (Exodus 5–11). The innermost frame in this menorah pattern continues with the consecration of the first-born in Israel to Yahweh (13:1–16). And in the center we find the institution of the Festival of Passover in ancient Israel (Exodus 12).

The section on the journey of the people of Israel from the crossing of *Yam Suf* (Sea of Reeds) to the war with Amalek at Rephidim may be outlined in a menorah pattern:

Journey from the Sea-Crossing to Rephidim	*Exod 15:20–17:16*
A Miriam's song—beginning of the wars of Yahweh	15:20–21
B Marah—bitter water made sweet ["I am Yahweh who heals"]	15:22–27
C Journey from Elim to the wilderness of Sin—no food	16:1–3
X **God's provision in the wilderness: manna and quail**	16:4–36
C´ Journey from the wilderness of Sin to Rephidim—no water	17:1
B´ Massah and Meribah—water from the rock	17:2–7
A´ Joshua and the war against Amalek [Yahweh's enemy]	17:8–16

The outer frame in this literary structure opens with a brief reference, on the part of Miriam, to Yahweh as a Divine Warrior who "has triumphed gloriously; the horse and his rider he has thrown into the sea" (15:21). It concludes with the account of the initial battle in the wars of Yahweh, which is fought under the leadership of Joshua, against the

Amalekites who subsequently become the traditional enemies of Yahweh (17:8–16). This literary unit begins and ends with fragments from the most ancient war songs in the Tanakh (15:21 and 17:16).

The account of the journey from *Yam Suf* (Sea of Reeds) to Mount Sinai is framed by parallel stories in which Yahweh produces water for his people in the wilderness—at Marah (15:22–26) and at Massah and Meribah (17:2–7). The journey is in two stages, which highlight the primary needs of God's people: food (15:27–16:3) and water (17:1). The focus of attention in the literary unit as a whole is God's miraculous provision of daily bread in the morning ("manna") and meat ("quails") in the evening (16:4–36). The provision of manna continues until the beginning of the second phase of the wars of Yahweh, when Joshua establishes the battle camp at Gilgal and the people observe the first Passover in the Promised Land (Josh 5:12).

Concept Check #8

Should Passover be observed as a regular part of the Christian calendar?

Check your answer at the back of this book.

---

b. Theophany and Covenant at Mount Sinai (Exodus 18–24)

The second "wheel" in Exodus may also be outlined in a menorah pattern:

Parashoth 17–18: Theophany and Covenant at Mount Sinai	*Exodus 18–24*
A Moses with his father-in-law Jethro, the priest of Midian	18:1–27
B Theophany on Mount Sinai—Ten Commandments (given orally)	19:1–20:17
C In fear, the people ask Moses to speak with God in their behalf	20:18–20
X **Theophany at Sinai—Moses meets God in thick darkness**	20:21
C´ Elaboration of 2nd Commandment—laws concerning worship	20:22–26
B´ Book of the Covenant—civil and criminal laws	21:1–23:33
A´ Theophany and covenant ceremony—Moses with the priests	24:1–18

The outermost frame here opens with a section on the visit of Jethro, "the priest of Midian, Moses' father-in-law" (18:1–27), and continues with a passage about Moses and the priests Aaron, Nadab, and Abihu on Mount Sinai (24:1–18). The second frame moves from the giving of the Ten Commandments (19:1–20:17), to the legislation commonly referred to as the "Book of the Covenant"—the oldest collection of civil and criminal laws in the Tanakh (Exodus 21–23). And in the center, the focus narrows to a single verse in which Moses enters "the thick darkness" where God is (20:21). Once again, we have a "riddle in the middle" for, as we know from 1 John 1:5, "God is light and in him is no darkness at all."

c. Covenant Broken and Renewed at Mount Sinai (Exodus 25–34)

The "third wheel," which is also the structural center of the Primary History (see section A of chapter 1 above), may be outlined here in a somewhat different menorah pattern, with its focus on Moses and Joshua together in the Meeting Tent:

Parashoth 19–21: Covenant Broken and Renewed at Mount Sinai	*Exodus 25–34*
A Yahweh reveals plans for the Tabernacle to house his presence	25:1–31:18
B Breaking of the covenant—Golden Calf, stone tablets shattered	32:1–35
C Yahweh speaks: I will not go with this "stiff-necked people"	33:1–6
X **Moses and Joshua in the Meeting Tent**	33:7–16
C´ Yahweh speaks: I will show you a glimpse of my glory	33:17–23
B´ Renewal of the covenant—with two new tablets of stone	34:1–28
A´ The shining face of Moses from being in Yahweh's presence	34:29–35

This section opens with a lengthy description of detailed plans for the Tabernacle that Yahweh commands Moses to build (25:1–31:18). The outermost frame concludes with a passage on the shining face of Moses, who "did not know that the skin of his face shone because he had been talking with God" (34:29). At the end of the book of Exodus, when Yahweh chooses to enter the completed structure, his glory fills the Tabernacle and Moses is no longer able to enter the Meeting Tent (40:34–35). The narrative content of the "third wheel" begins with the breaking of the covenant in the incident of the Golden Calf, when Moses shattered the two tablets of stone he received from God on the mountain (Exodus 32). The second frame concludes with the renewal of the covenant, with two new tablets of stone on which God writes once again the stipulations of the covenant agreement—the Ten Commandments (Exodus 34). And in the middle we find a complex riddle, as Moses asks Yahweh, "I pray thee, show me thy glory" (33:18). Yahweh grants his wish there on the holy mountain, at least in part, by allowing Moses to see his "goodness" as he passes by (34:19); but no one is permitted to see God himself and live (34:20).

d. Establishing Israel's Worship in the Tabernacle (Exodus 35–40)

For the most part, the "fourth wheel" repeats the content of Exodus 25–31. What is presented in the former context as plans to build the Tabernacle become a detailed record of how those plans are carried out—in the construction of the Tabernacle and the establishment of the religion of ancient Israel.

Parashoth 22–23: Establishing the Tabernacle Religion of Israel	*Exodus 35–40*
A Preparations for making the Tabernacle and request for offerings	35:1–29
B Bezalel and Oholiab chosen as craftsmen—people give too much	35:30–36:7
C Construction of the Tabernacle	36:8–38
X **Making the furnishings and the altar of burnt offering**	37:1–38:8
C´ Making the court of the Tabernacle	38:9–20
B´ Work of Bezalel and Oholiab with inventory of materials used	38:21–39:31
A´ Work completed—erection and furnishing of the Tabernacle	39:32–40:38

On the one hand, preparations are made for building the Tabernacle, including a request for offerings from the people (35:1–29). At the conclusion of this section, we have the completion of the work, climaxed by the erection and furnishing of the Tabernacle (39:32–39:31). The skill of the craftsmen Bezalel and Oholiab is described in parallel passages, as the second frame focuses on the materials used in the construction of the Tabernacle. The third frame moves from construction of the Tabernacle (36:8–38), to the making of the court of the Tabernacle. And in the center we find the description of the table, lampstand (menorah), altars, anointing oil, and the construction of the altar of burnt offering as its climax (38:9–20). The architecture and furnishings of the Tabernacle will be taken up in quite a different manner in the book of Leviticus, as we will see in chapter 3 below.

2. The Establishment of Moses as Israel's Leader (Exodus 1–24)

The "Moses Story" begins with an introductory note that takes the reader four hundred years in time in the space of seven verses—from the death of Joseph who "was put in a coffin in Egypt" (Gen 50:26) to the setting for the birth of Moses.

a. From Twelve Sons of Jacob to a Microcosm of the Nations   Exod 1:1–7

A	These are the names of the *children of Israel* [cf. Gen 46:8–27]	1:1a
B	They came to Egypt with Jacob, each with his household	1:1b
C	Eleven of the twelve sons of Jacob are listed by name	1:2–4
X	**The offspring of Jacob were seventy persons** [cf. Genesis 10]	1:5a
C´	Joseph was already in Egypt	1:5b
B´	Then Joseph died and all that generation	1:6
A´	The *children of Israel* were fruitful and multiplied [cf. Gen 1:28, 9:1–2]	1:7

The framework in this menorah pattern moves back through the book of Genesis. The list of "the names of the children of Israel who came to Egypt with Jacob, each with his household" (1:1) is spelled out in detail in Gen 46:8–27. The list includes "seventy persons" (1:5a), which reminds the reader of the Table of Nations in Genesis 10. The unit concludes with specific reference to the first three commands given to Adam and Eve in Genesis 1:28 and again to Noah, "Be fruitful and multiply, and fill the earth" (Gen 9:1). The remaining commands to subdue the earth and to have dominion over it are not appropriate to a story of slaves in Egypt. The fulfillment of those commands will await another chapter at a later point in time.

b. The Children of Israel in Egypt   Exodus 1

A	The children of Israel have increased in the land of Egypt	1:1–7
B	A new king appears who does not know Joseph	1:8
C	Pharaoh decides to "deal shrewdly with them"—as slave laborers	1:9–11
X	**The more God's people are oppressed, the more they increase**	1:12
C´	Pharaoh's "final solution"—every male child born must die	1:13–14
B´	Two Hebrew midwives (Shiphrah and Puah) outwit Pharaoh	1:15–21
A´	Every boy that is born to the Hebrews must be cast into the Nile	1:22

Moses' mother (identified as Jochebed in Exod 6:20) obeys the wicked decree of Pharaoh, at least in one sense. She is ordered to cast her infant son into the Nile, and so she does—after placing him in an "ark" (*tebah*). The Hebrew word for "ark" here is the word used earlier of

Noah's "ark" in Genesis 6–9. That "ark" was a vessel God used to save the human race from the waters of chaos and destruction in the Great Flood. The "ark" here is a vessel God is using once again to deliver Moses, and through him ultimately the whole human race once again, from the waters of chaos and death. But this time there is something new added to the story—the *naming* of Moses. After all this is the *Book of Names*!

c. The Call of Moses at the Burning Bush   Exodus 1–4

A	The children of Israel in Egypt—oppressed by hard service	1:1–14
B	The "power" of two midwives who outwit Pharaoh	1:15–22
C	The naming of Moses by the daughter of Pharaoh	2:1–25
X	Theophany of the bush—the call of Moses	3:1–12
C´	The name of Yahweh is revealed to Moses	3:13–15
B´	Moses' miraculous powers—his rod and sign of the leprous hand	4:1–17
A´	Moses returns to Egypt, Yahweh has seen their affliction (4:31)	4:18–31

The children of Israel were powerless in the face of a ruthless tyrant who was oppressing them. The Egyptians "made the children of Israel to *serve* with rigor. And they made their lives bitter with hard *service*, in mortar and brick, and in all kinds of *service* in the field; in all their *service* they made them *serve* with rigor" (1:13–14). The reiterative effect of the five-fold use of the verb "to serve" drums home the reality of their drudgery in slavery. Though the Hebrew midwives appear to be powerless, they manage to outwit Pharaoh in his diabolical plot to kill the newborn children of Israel (1:15–22). Moses' miraculous powers demonstrate God's grace and foreshadow miracles yet to come in the story (4:1–17). The innermost frame in this menorah pattern includes parallel incidents on the theme of names. Pharaoh's daughter names Moses (Exodus 2), and Yahweh reveals his name to Moses at the burning bush (Exodus 3). The Hebrew word used for bush (*seneh*) foreshadows the geographical location of Sinai, where Moses will receive further revelation on a mountain wrapped in smoke and burning with a mysterious fire (19:16–18, 24:17). The focus of attention in this menorah pattern is on Moses' call to return to Egypt, for Yahweh has seen the affliction of his chosen people (4:31).

d. The Naming of Moses   Exodus 1–3

A	Twelve "children of Israel" (listed by name) become a vast multitude	1:1–7
B	Israelites struggle in forced labor and oppression	1:8–22
C	Birth and infancy of Moses—he is "cast into the Nile"	2:1–9
X	Pharaoh's daughter names the child "Moses"	2:10
C´	Moses as an adult—flight from Egypt, marriage, family in Midian	2:11–22
B´	Israelites groan in slavery and cry out; God takes notice of them	2:23–25
A´	God reveals his name to Moses at the burning bush	3:13–15

Moses is named by Pharaoh's daughter with this explanation: "Because I drew him out of the water" (2:10). It appears that this unnamed Egyptian princess does not know the Hebrew language very well, though she does know enough to identify the name of Moses with the correct verbal root in Hebrew (*mashah* means "to draw out or from"). As an Egyptian, she also knows that these same sounds in her native tongue mean "son of" (as in Ramses = "son of [the god] Ra" or Thutmoses = "son of [the god] Thoth"). In her attempt to name the child, she chooses a participle, but she uses the wrong grammatical form—or does she? The passive participle, which would fit her description of one "who is drawn from" the waters would have been "Mashuy"; but she names him with the active participle *Mosheh*. Unwittingly she names him correctly as the one "who draws forth"—a foreshadowing of the child's destiny. He will draw the people of God through the waters of chaos and death in the Exodus from Egypt in the pages that follow.

Exodus 2:11–25 picks up the story forty years later, when Moses impulsively kills an Egyptian who is mistreating a Hebrew slave. As a result of this rash act of misdirected leadership, Moses is forced to flee into the wilderness for forty years where God teaches him more about leadership than he ever learned in the palace schools of Egypt.

e. Moses Spends Forty Years in the Wilderness   Exod 2:11–25

A	Moses sees the forced labor of the people	2:11
B	Moses kills an Egyptian and subsequently flees to Midian	2:12–15
C	Seven daughters of Jethro come to a well to water their flock	2:16
X	**An Egyptian *drew water* for us and watered the flock**	2:17–19
C´	Moses marries Zipporah, one of the seven daughters of Jethro	2:20–21
B´	Zipporah's son is named Gershom—"I was an alien there"	2:22
A´	God sees their groaning and he took notice of them	2:23–25

Moses' action in "drawing water" for Midianite shepherd girls foreshadows once again what God is calling him to do in the meaning of his name. The second period of forty years in the life of Moses comes to an end when God calls Moses to leadership at the burning bush. Fire is a symbol of God's purity, and a reminder to Moses that he is standing on holy ground (3:5). God has not forgotten his people who are suffering in the fires of persecution. He will use Moses to deliver them from the furnace of affliction.

f. Yahweh Summons Moses to Go Back to Egypt   Exodus 3:16–4:31

A	Moses is told to meet with the elders of Israel in Egypt	3:16–22
B	Yahweh equips Moses with miraculous signs and a spokesman	4:1–17
C	Moses gets Jethro's permission for him to return to Egypt	4:18
X	**Yahweh told Moses to go back to Egypt**	4:19
C´	Moses takes his family and leaves for Egypt (with the staff of God)	4:20–23
B´	Yahweh tries to kill Moses—"the bridegroom of blood"	4:24–26
A´	Moses and Aaron meet with the elders of Israel in Egypt	4:27–31

Moses' response to God's self-disclosure and call is a stream of excuses:

> ➤ questioning his own ability: "Who am I?" (3:11)

> ➤ questioning his authority: "What shall I say to them?" (3:13)

> ➤ questioning the people's response: "They will not believe me." (4:1)

> ➤ questioning his eloquence: "I am slow of speech and of a slow tongue." (4:10)

God has an answer for each excuse; for the real issue is the simple fact that Moses does not want to go (4:13). God does not command us to go 'gainst our will; he just makes us willing to go!

g. The Contest between Yahweh and Pharaoh   Exodus 5–13

A   Pharaoh's show of strength—make bricks without straw   5:1–23
B   Yahweh's deliverance of Israel assured—Yahweh's word   6:1–13
C   Genealogy of Moses and Aaron   6:14–25
X   **Moses and Aaron speak to Pharaoh**   6:26–7:5
C´   Moses is 80 and Aaron 83 when they obey Yahweh   7:6–7
B´   Sign of Yahweh's deliverance—Aaron's miraculous rod   7:8–13
A´ Yahweh's show of strength—ten plagues and pillars of cloud/fire 7:14–13:22

In the contest, Pharaoh displays defiance by ordering the slaves to make bricks without straw (Exodus 5). The following chapters present a series of ten plagues in Egypt (Exodus 7–13) and the display of Yahweh's awesome power in the pillars of cloud and fire before the crossing of the sea. The plagues are designed to answer Pharaoh's question in 5:2—"Who is Yahweh, that I should obey his voice?" They function as a seminar—"Theology 101"—to teach Pharaoh that Yahweh is God (cf. 7:17 and 8:10), for each of the plagues is directed at an object that the Egyptians revere as deity.

Numerous students of the Bible have noted a logical progression in the first nine plagues. As Flinders Petrie put it in 1911, "The order of the plagues was the natural order of such troubles on a lesser scale in the Egyptian seasons, as was pointed out long ago."[2]

h. The Ten Plagues—Yahweh's Delivering Presence   Exod 7:8–11:10

A Pharaoh's heart is hardened in face of God's sign with Aaron's rod   7:8–13
B   Three plagues—repulsive conditions: blood, frogs, lice   7:14–8:19
C   Fourth plague: flies   8:20–24
X   **Pharoah speaks: "Go, sacrifice to your God within the land"** 8:25–32
C´   Fifth and Sixth plagues: murrain[3] and boils   9:1–12
B´   Three plagues—physical disasters: hail, locusts, darkness   9:13–10:29
A´ Pharaoh's heart is hardened in the face of all these wonders   11:1–10

The institution of Passover is recounted in Exodus 12, where the redemption of the people is expressed symbolically. Provision is made of a lamb without blemish (12:5), which is to be slain before sundown (12:6). The shed blood of this lamb is applied to the doorposts and the lintel over the door of each house, so that the "angel of death" will "pass over" that particular home in God's tenth and final judgment.

i. Passover as the Climax to the Ten Plagues   Exodus 11–12

A Warning of the final plague, then Pharaoh will drive you out   11:1–10
B   The first Passover is instituted   12:1–13
C   Observe the Festival of Unleavened Bread   12:14–28
X   **The tenth plague—death of the first-born**   12:29–32
C´   They took unleavened dough and journeyed to Succoth   12:33–42
B´   Directions for observing Passover   12:43–49
A´ Yahweh brings Israel out of Egypt, company by company   12:50–51

---

2   See W. M. F. Petrie, *Egypt and Israel* (London, 1911).

3   A disease that afflicted cattle.

The relationship of the Passover ritual to the work of Yeshua the Messiah (Jesus Christ) is evident in 1 Cor 5:7, which states that "Christ, our paschal lamb, has been sacrificed." Yeshua is "the Lamb of God, who takes away the sin of the world" (John 1:29), who is "without blemish or spot" (1 Peter 1:9). His blood was shed on Mount Golgotha, outside the walls of ancient Jerusalem, so that all peoples everywhere might escape the final judgment. And once again, the provision for deliverance through the blood of Yeshua must be applied in a personal way to be effective.

The account of Exod 13:1–16 stands as a memorial to future generations who look back to what happened on "this day." They are to consecrate the first-born "among the people of Israel, both of man and of beast" (13:2). In time to come, the people are commanded to "set apart to the Lord all that first opens the womb . . . Every first-born of man among your sons you shall redeem" (13:12–13).

j. Crossing the Sea and the Song of Moses   Exodus 14–15

A	Crossing the Sea—Pharaoh's chariots pursue them into the sea	14:1–25
B	The pursuers drowned	14:26–31
C	Yahweh's triumph: "horse and rider he has thrown into the sea"	15:1–10
X	Question: "Who is like you, O Yahweh?"	15:11
C´	Yahweh's triumph: "you guided them . . . to your holy abode"	15:12–18
B´	The pursuers (horses and chariots) caught in waters	15:19
A´	Song of Miriam: "horse and rider he has thrown into the sea"	15:20–21

The series of crises in the wilderness of Exodus 14–18 includes the most central redemptive act of God in the Tanakh—the crossing of the "Sea of Reeds" (*Yam Suf*, often interpreted as the Red Sea). The miracle at the Sea is to the people of God in the First Testament what the empty tomb is to the people of God in the Second Testament. God leads the "children of Israel" out of Egypt in a way that makes it virtually impossible for them to ever go back to Egypt. In Exod 14:10–14, they find themselves facing *Yam Suf* (Sea of Reeds) with the Egyptian army in hot pursuit. There is nothing to do but to "Stand still, and see the salvation of Yahweh" (14:13).

Scholars remain divided on the precise location of this "Crossing of the Red Sea" and its date in history. Most opt for a crossing somewhere in the vicinity of the Suez Canal through the "Sea of Reeds" and a date of either 1450–1440 BCE or 1290–1225 BCE.

k. God's Provision of Bread and Water in the Wilderness   Exod 15:20–17:16

A	Song of Miriam—beginning of the wars of Yahweh	15:20–21
B	Marah—bitter water made sweet ["I am Yahweh who heals"]	15:22–26
C	From Elim to the wilderness of Sin—no food	15:27–16:3
X	Manna—bread in the wilderness	16:4–36
C´	From the wilderness of Sin to Rephidim—no water	17:1
B´	Massah and Meribah—water from the rock	17:2–7
A´	Joshua and the war with Amalek	17:8–16

The material provision of food and water in the wilderness foreshadows the portrayal of Yeshua the Messiah as the "bread from heaven" (John 6:32–35) and the "water of life"

(1 Cor 10:4). The manna of Exodus 16 is a striking example of the way God supplies our needs:

> ➤ day by day—we depend on God one day at a time
> ➤ sufficient for our needs—there is always enough
> ➤ completely satisfying—nothing else is needed

l. God Establishes His Covenant with the People of Israel   Exod 17:8–24:14

The military crisis of Exodus 17 introduces the Amalekites who become the traditional "enemy of the Jews" throughout the Tanakh (cf. Haman "the Agagite" in the story of Esther). Moses intercedes for Israel on a mountaintop while God gives Joshua the victory in the valley below. This is the first reference to Joshua in the Bible, which foreshadows what is to come in the second phase of the wars of Yahweh. The defeat of Pharaoh's army in the Exodus from Egypt under Moses' leadership is the first phase of the wars of Yahweh, which concludes with the conquest of the two Amorite kings (Sihon and Og) in Transjordan. Joshua is the leader for the second phase of the wars of Yahweh, which we refer to as the Eisodus (entry into the Promised Land).

In Exodus 18, Moses takes the first step toward the institutionalization of authority so far as leadership in ancient Israel is concerned. At the suggestion of his father-in-law Jethro, he delegates responsibility to able men in Israel (18:25). As Aaron Wildavsky has noted, Jethro's advice here "comprises what have become classical principles of public administration."[4]

m. God Reveals Himself to Moses and Joshua   Exod 17:8–24:14

A	Joshua and the war with Amalek	17:8–16
B	Jethro's visit	18:1–27
C	Theophany: Moses brought the people out to meet God	19:1–25
X	**Revelation: Ten Commandments and Book of the Covenant**	20:1–23:33
C′	Theophany: Moses brought Aaron and other leaders to "see" God	24:1–8
B′	Moses with Aaron, Nadab, Abihu and 70 elders on Mount Sinai	24:9–11
A′	Joshua with Moses on Mount Sinai	24:12–14

The experience of Moses on the mountain with God began three days after the crossing of *Yam Suf* (Sea of Reeds), when the people of Israel first "encamped before the mountain" (19:2). The "words" that Yahweh instructs Moses to bring down from the mountain are addressed to the people: "you shall be my own possession among all the peoples . . . and you shall be to me a kingdom of priests and a holy nation" (19:5–6). Three days later "Moses brought the people out of the camp to meet God; and they took their stand at the foot of the mountain" (19:17). Moses ascends the mountain once again, where he is told to "Go down, and come up bringing Aaron with you" (19:24). In the second theophany (20:18–26), "the people stood afar off, while Moses drew near to the thick darkness where God was" (19:21), but no mention is made of Aaron being there. In between these two theophanies stands the first giving of the Ten Commandments, which are not yet written on tablets of stone (see Exod 24:12).

---

4   A. Wildavsky, "From Equity to Hierarchy: The Institutionalization of Leadership," in *The Nursing Father: Moses as a Political Leader* (Univ. of Alabama Press, 1984), pp. 123-151 (quotation from p. 146).

Once Israel becomes a free nation it is imperative that they have a detailed code of laws by which to order their lives in the Promised Land. God supplies this need with the Mosaic covenant. That covenant is established within the context of divine revelation on Mount Sinai—in three parts. For the third theophany in the sequence here (Exodus 24), Moses is told to bring "Aaron, Nadab, Abihu, and seventy of the elders of Israel" (24:10 with him, though "Moses alone shall come near to Yahweh" (24:2). Before ascending the mountain with his companions, "Moses wrote all the words of Yahweh" (24:4). Afterwards, "Moses and Aaron, Nadab, and Abihu, and seventy of the elders of Israel went up, and they saw the God of Israel . . . they beheld God, and ate and drank" (24:9–11). This is a remarkable scene in light of what is said later in another theophany on Mount Sinai (cf. Exod 33:20–23).

A recitation of legal injunctions, often called the Book of the Covenant (or the Covenant Code, Exodus 21–23), stands between the second and third theophanic visitations and corresponds to the oral presentation of the Ten Commandments in Exod 20: 1–17. The actual writing of the Ten Commandments on tablets of stone takes place later during the third theophany on the mountain, after Moses leaves the others and ascends further (24:12–13). The fact that Moses takes Joshua with him at this point is interesting; for there is no mention of Joshua's presence on Mount Sinai up to this point in the narrative (24:13, cf. 33:11). "The glory of Yahweh settled on Mount Sinai, and the cloud covered it six days; and on the seventh day he called to Moses out of the midst of the cloud. Now the appearance of Yahweh was like a devouring fire on the top of the mountain in the sight of the people of Israel . . . And Moses was on the mountain forty days and forty nights" (24:16–18).

In Exodus 19–24, the Mosaic covenant is ratified and regulated. It is important that we understand the purpose of the Mosaic law within this context. Yeshua makes it clear that he did not intend to do away with the Mosaic law as such. He came "to fulfill it" (see Matt 5:17)—that is, to enable us to order our lives in terms of the eternal aspects of the Mosaic covenant through the power of the new life available through Yeshua the Messiah (Jesus Christ). When Yeshua refers to the Ten Commandments in the Sermon on the Mount with the familiar words, "You have heard that it was said . . . but I say to you," he is correcting the common interpretation of these laws prevalent at that moment in Judaism. He is not challenging the original meaning of the law of Moses. In fact, his interpretation is aimed at setting forth the true meaning of the Mosaic covenant; for the law was never the means of salvation. As Paul once put it, "the law was put in charge to lead us to Christ that we might be justified by faith" (Gal 3:24). Abraham and all the other heroes of the faith after him in the Tanakh were justified by faith—the same as the rest of us, exactly as Hebrews 11 tells us. The only difference is that they saw "through a glass darkly" while we have the privilege of seeing "face to face" (1 Cor 13:12).

The content of the Ten Commandments falls into two major divisions: the first four outline our responsibility to God and the last six our responsibility to fellow human beings. This is essentially how Yeshua summarizes the Ten Commandments when he says that the law is summarized in the statement that we should love God and love our neighbor (Luke 10:27–28). The first half of this statement sums up the first four commandments and the second half summarizes the remaining six commandments. Two important lessons can be drawn from this analysis: the epitome of the law is *love*; and the last six duties will only be fulfilled if we recognize our responsibility in the first four. Only when we are in proper relationship with God can we fulfill our responsibilities to fellow human beings. Those six responsibilities according to Exodus 20:12–17 are as follows:

- ➤ honor your father and your mother
- ➤ you shall not murder
- ➤ you shall not commit adultery
- ➤ you shall not steal
- ➤ you shall not give false testimony
- ➤ you shall not covet your neighbor's property

The best commentary on what these laws mean is found in Matt 5:17–48. The legalism prevalent within Judaism in Yeshua's day had robbed these great principles of much of their power in terms of shaping our daily lives. Yeshua restores the law to its rightful place of authority in governing right relationships between human beings here on this earth.

Concept Check #9

Are the Ten Commandments still binding for followers of Yeshua (Jesus) today? If so, what is our responsibility to the Law as practiced in ancient Israel?

Check your answer at the back of this book.

---

3. Yahweh's Tabernacling Presence in Israel's Midst (Exodus 25–40)

Though Exodus 25–40 is often summarized under the title "The Tabernacle," this is misleading. It is true that the bulk of material here deals with detailed plans to build the Tabernacle (Exodus 25–31) and its actual construction (Exodus 35–40), but the matters of central importance are merely framed by these large blocks of material. In fact, the central chapters of Exodus 32–34 stand in the structural center of the Primary History as a whole (i.e., the Torah and the Prophets in Jewish tradition).

a. The Glory of Yahweh Fills the Tabernacle (Exod 24:15–18 and 40:34–38)

The second half of the book of Exodus is introduced with a brief note, which is arranged in the form of an inversion (24:15–18):

A   Then Moses went up on the mountain and the cloud covered the mountain
B   The *glory of Yahweh* settled on Mount Sinai, and the cloud covered it for six days;
X   On the 7th day (Yahweh) called to Moses out of the cloud.
B´   The appearance of the *glory of Yahweh* was like a devouring fire
      on the top of the mountain in the sight of the people of Israel.
A´ Moses entered the cloud, and went up on the mountain.
    Moses was on the mountain for forty days and forty nights. [Exod 24:15–18]

This unit forms an envelope with a similar one at the conclusion of the book of Exodus (40:34–38).

A   Then the cloud covered the Meeting Tent, and the *glory of Yahweh* filled the Tabernacle.

B   Moses was not able to enter the Meeting Tent because the cloud settled upon it,
       and the *glory of Yahweh* filled the Tabernacle.

X   **Whenever the cloud was taken up from the Tabernacle,**
            the Israelites would set out <u>on each stage of their journey</u>.

B´   But if the cloud was not taken up, then they did not set out until the day that it was
         taken up.

A´   For the cloud of Yahweh was on the Tabernacle by day, and fire was in the cloud by night,
         before the eyes of all the house of Israel <u>at each stage of their journey</u>.   [Exod 40:34–38]

The appearance of Yahweh on the seventh day suggests that the previous six days are a time of preparation. In short, we find in 24:15–16 a reflection of Genesis 1, with six days of "creation" followed by the Sabbath rest. The concluding section in 40:34–38 anticipates the journey from Mount Sinai to the Promised Land in the book of Numbers.

b. The Promised Presence of Yahweh on Mount Sinai (Exodus 32–34)

As we have already noted, the section between the design of the Tabernacle (25:1–31:11) and its construction (35:4–40:33) constitutes the center of the Primary History (Genesis through 2 Kings). The content of this pivotal section in the center of the second half of Exodus may be outlined in a menorah pattern:

The Center of the Primary History in a Menorah Pattern	*Exod 31:12–35:3*
A The Sabbath law	31:12–17
B The two stone tablets of the covenant	31:18
C The Golden Calf incident—covenant broken	32:1–33:6
X **The tent outside the camp—the cloud and Yahweh's glory**	33:7–23
C´ Moses makes new tablets—covenant renewed	34:1–28
B´ The shining face of Moses ("with the two tablets, 34:29)	34:29–35
A´ Sabbath regulations	35:1–3

Once again we find an example of the "riddle in the middle" with a mysterious text in the center of this menorah pattern. The text says, "Moses used to take the tent and pitch it outside the camp, far from the camp; and he called it the Meeting Tent" (32:7). When the Tabernacle complex is constructed, this tent takes its place within it—in the center of the camp. The text goes on to say, "When Moses entered the tent, the pillar of cloud would descend and stand at the entrance of the tent . . . and Yahweh used to speak to Moses face to face, as one speaks to a friend" (33:9–11). One of these personal conversations follows, in which Moses makes an amazing request: "Show me your glory, I pray" (33:18). Yahweh tells Moses that he will give him a glimpse of his presence from the safety of a cave on the mountain. Yahweh says, "while my glory passes by I will put you in a cleft of the rock, and I will cover you with my hand, and you shall see my back; but my face shall not be seen" (33:22). At the conclusion of the book of Exodus that glory fills the Tabernacle.

The episode of the Golden Calf, which takes place at the foot of Mount Sinai while Moses was receiving the first copy of the two stone tablets containing the Ten Commandments in Exodus 32, is instructive. The text presents three great sins on the part of the people and Aaron, who submitted to their demands:

> ➤ Impatience—the people tire of waiting for Moses and God (32:1)

> ➤ Idolatry—shaping of the Golden Calf violates the first two commandments (32:2–6)

> ➤ Irresponsibility—Aaron denies responsibility for his sin (32:21–24)

In typical fashion, Aaron puts the blame on someone else. After all, as he puts it, "I threw (the gold) into the fire, and there came out this calf" (32:24). Like Adam and Eve in the Garden of Eden, Aaron does not want to accept responsibility for his actions. At this point a fourth item is added to the list of sins, namely the intercession of Moses to deal with the consequences.

The conversation between Moses and Yahweh about the people's sin highlights a note of humor in Exodus 32 as Moses and Yahweh have a dispute about the children of Israel. While Moses is still on the mountain, Yahweh says, "Go down, for *your people, whom you brought out of the land of Egypt*, have corrupted themselves" (32:7). A few verses later Moses responds, "O Yahweh, why does your wrath burn hot against *your people whom you brought out of the land of Egypt with great power and with a mighty hand*" (32:11)? It appears that neither party wishes to claim ownership of this wayward people.

This pivotal chapter concludes with the report that Yahweh "sent a plague upon the people, because they made the calf—the one that Aaron made" (32:35). In some respects, the narrative picks up again in 34:1 with Yahweh commanding Moses to go back up the mountain to receive a second copy of the Ten Commandments written on stone tablets. In between these two passages we find a complex chapter, which constitutes the structural center of the Primary History as a whole.

Exod 33:11 marks a "watershed" in the biblical narrative; for the experience of God through Joshua and his successors will be different from that of Moses. Moses experienced the presence of Yahweh "face to face, as a man speaks to a friend" (33:11a). Joshua and his successors will be more removed from the presence of God, and dependent on either the Meeting Tent or perhaps a new kind of experience altogether, which Elijah will have at a decisive moment in the Special History of the covenant people of God (1 Kings 19). This matter is taken up in detail later in *The Former Prophets*. In some respects, the experience of Moses on Mount Sinai anticipates this experience on the part of Elijah with its reference to the fact that God is to be found in "the thick darkness" (Exod 20:21). For Elijah, God will reveal himself in "awesome silence" (1 Kings 19:12).

The experience of Moses in a cave on Mount Sinai, where he manages to get a glimpse of God's glory as he passes by (33:21–23), anticipates other theophanies to come on this same mountain. Elijah experiences the mysterious presence of Yahweh here in 1 Kings 19 and, in the transfiguration of Yeshua, when both Moses and Elijah are present, the mysterious glory of God is revealed in the fullness of time (Matt 17:1–8, Mark 9:2–8 and Luke 9:28–36).

> ### Concept Check #10
> Why does Joshua appear at the structural center of Exodus 33?
> Check your answer at the back of this book.

c. The Tabernacle Designed and Constructed (Exodus 25–31 and 35–40)

Exodus 35–40 presents the construction of the Tabernacle according to the plans received in chapters 25–31. For this project to be successful, two things are necessary: right materials (35:4–9) and skilled, reliable workers (35:10–36:7). Moses requests that those of "a willing heart" (35:5) and "a wise heart" (35:10) bring freewill offerings for the construction. The response is so enthusiastic that Moses subsequently orders the people to refrain from bringing any more (36:6–7). The workers chosen to build the Tabernacle are supernaturally endowed [i.e., "filled with the Holy Spirit" (35:31)] and naturally skilled (35:35). When the construction is completed, "the glory of Yahweh filled the Tabernacle" (40:34) such that even Moses is no longer able to enter the Meeting Tent (40:35).

The account of the construction of the Tabernacle in Exodus 35–40 may be outlined in a nested menorah pattern, as follows:

The Tabernacle Complex Constructed	*Exodus 35–40*
A Sabbath law—restricts work on the Tabernacle	35:1–3
B Preparations for constructing the Tabernacle	35:4–19
C Offerings for building the Tabernacle	35:20–29
X **Bezalel and Oholiab build the Tabernacle complex**	35:30–38:20
C´ Materials of the Tabernacle and making vestments for the priests	38:21–39:31
B´ The work is completed—"And Moses blessed them"	39:32–43
A´ Erection and furnishing of the Tabernacle (on 1st day of 1st month)	40:1–38

2nd Level Menorah: Building of the Tabernacle Complex	*Exod 35:30–38:20*
A Bezalel and Oholiab chosen as craftsmen—people give too much	35:30–36:7
B Construction of the Tabernacle	36:8–38
C Inside furnishings: ark, table, lampstand, incense altar, oil	37:1–29
X **Altar of burnt offering**	38:1–7
C´ Outside furnishings: bronze laver, pillars, hangings, bases, pegs	38:8–20
B´ Making the court of the Tabernacle	38:9–20
A´ Work of Bezalel and Oholiab with inventory of materials used	38:21–39:31

The concentric structure narrows to a focus on the work of the chosen craftsmen, Bezalel and Oholiab, and to the altar of burnt offering in particular. That altar becomes the center of worship in ancient Israel.

D. The Tabernacle in the Religion of Israel

The Tabernacle was intended to be a model of Mount Sinai—the place where God is known in human experience. In terms of spatial design, there are three parts in the tabernacle complex—with gradations of holiness: the outer court, the Holy Place, and the Holy of Holies. The same is true of Mount Sinai. The people of Israel assembled at the foot of the mountain, and the priests were allowed to go with Moses on the mountain itself; but Moses alone went to the top of mountain "to the thick darkness where God was" (20:21). The wording here describes the Holy of Holies in the Meeting Tent, for the inner sanctum of the Meeting Tent had no windows and the sacred ark of the covenant with the Ten Commandments written on two tablets of stone was housed in utter darkness. With this imagery in mind, it is easier to understand the description of the communal meal shared by Moses, Aaron, Nadab, Abihu, and seventy elders of Israel on Mount Sinai in Exod 24:9–11. When the text says, "they saw the God of Israel; and there under his feet as it were a pavement of sapphire stone, like the very heaven for clearness," they were describing the experience of the priests in the Holy Place of Yahweh's sanctuary. God's presence was "seen" through the veil, which separated them from the Holy of Holies. The text says, "they beheld God, and ate and drank" (24:11). But Moses alone was privileged to enter the Holy of Holies symbolically, on the summit of Mount Sinai, where he saw God and spoke with him "face to face, as a man speaks to his friend" (33:11).

The tabernacle complex may be described as a tent within a tent. The Meeting Tent, which is a structure consisting of two rooms, the Holy Place and the Holy of Holies, is made of a framework covered by two tapestry curtains. The entrance is covered with a fabric screen, and another screen (or veil) inside the Meeting Tent separates the two rooms.

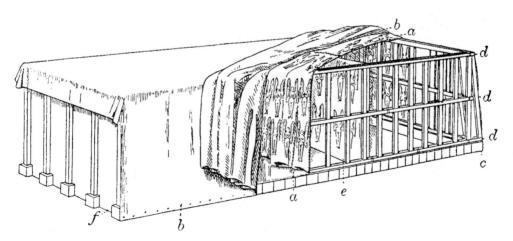

Model of the Meeting Tent, as reconstructed by Prof. Kennedy
The two outermost coverings (Exod 26:14) are removed, showing the framework covered by the tapesty covering *a a* with the figures of cherubim, the goat's hair covering of the "tent" (26:7) *b b*, one of the corner frames *c*, the horizontal "bars" *d d d*, the veil *e*, and the screen *f*.

The Meeting Tent is located in the western half of a larger open air "tent" (the Tabernacle), which measures 100 cubits by 50 cubits (approximately 150 x 75 feet). The eastern half of the interior of the Tabernacle is a perfect square measuring 50 cubits on each side. The Meeting Tent is arranged so that the Ark of the Covenant (inside the Holy of Holies) is in the center of the western half of the Tabernacle. The altar of burnt offering is in the center of the eastern half—opposite the entrance to the Meeting Tent.

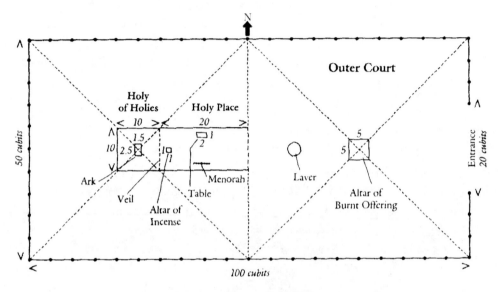

The Tabernacle of Ancient Israel
All numbers within the rectangle refer to cubits.
[Source: Sarna, *JPS Torah Commentary: Exodus* (1991), p. 155]

Worshipers in ancient Israel brought their sacrificial offerings to the outer court of the Tabernacle, which were presented to Yahweh by the Levitical priests on the altar of burnt offering in the center of the court, opposite the Meeting Tent. Between the altar of burnt offering and the Meeting Tent stands the laver, which the priests use for ceremonial ablutions in their priestly duties.

The screen on the eastern end of the Meeting Tent separates the worshipers from the Holy Place, where the Levitical priests do their work. That room contains three items of furniture: a table on the northern side, on which the priests place holy bread (the bread of the Presence) and sacred vessels. Opposite the table stands the golden menorah (lampstand). And in front of the veil separating the Holy Place from the Holy of Holies stands a golden altar for the burning of incense. A "veil" separates the two rooms of the Meeting Tent. The Ark of the Covenant, which contains the two stone tablets with the Ten Commandments, is in the center of the Holy of Holies, beneath two golden cherubim, which in antiquity were

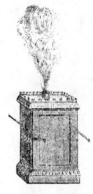

Incense Altar

normally adornments of a throne. Yahweh is the invisible king enthroned in "thick darkness" upon his battle palladium, the Ark of the Covenant.

The instructions for building the altar for burnt offering may be outlined in a menorah pattern:

Instructions for Building the Altar for Burnt Offering	*Exod 27:1–8*
A Make the altar of acacia wood overlaid with bronze (5 x 5 x 3 cubits)	27:1
B Make horns for it on its four corners	27:2
C Make its utensils: pots, shovels, basins, forks and fire-pans	27:3
X **Make a bronze grating with bronze rings at its four corners**	27:4
C′ Put the grating under the ledge of the altar	27:5
B′ Make poles to put through the bronze rings—to carry the altar	27:6–7
A′ Make the altar hollow, with boards—as shown on the mountain	27:8

The priests step up on the ledge of the altar to perform their duties; for, in Lev 9:22, we read that Aaron *"came down* from offering the sin offering" on the altar.

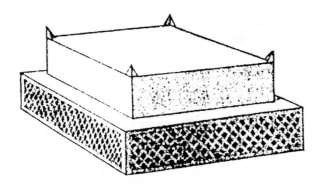

Altar of Burnt Offering

The menorah (lampstand) was hammered out of a single ingot of "pure gold." Extending from the central shaft on either side were three branches, each one ornamented after the flower of the almond tree. The menorah pattern dominates the Hebrew text, which has the structure of "wheels within wheels"—all of them with the same seven-part structure. The description of the instructions for building the Tabernacle in Exodus 25–31 is in six parts, each of which is introduced by the words, "Yahweh said to Moses." The content of Exodus 25–31 may be outlined in a menorah pattern, as follows:

The Golden Menorah

Instructions for Building the Tabernacle Complex   *Exodus 25–31*

A	Yahweh requests an offering from the people to build the Tabernacle	25:1–30:10
B	A tax is levied for the support of the sanctuary	30:11–16
C	Instructions to build the laver of bronze for ritual ablutions	30:17–21
X	**Formula for holy anointing oil—to consecrate the priests**	30:22–33
C´	The formula is given for the incense to burn on the altar of incense	30:34–38
B´	Appointment of craftsmen to do the work (Bezalel and Oholiab)	31:1–11
A´	Yahweh commands the people to keep the Sabbath [4th Commandment]	31:12–18

Instructions for building the Tabernacle (Exodus 25–31) are in six sections, which are marked by the words "Yahweh said to Moses" (25:1, 30:11, 30:17, 30:22, 30:34 and 31:1). The seventh section here is the Sabbath law in 31:12–18, which suggests that the underlying structural pattern is the seven days of creation in Genesis 1:1–2:3. The building of the Tabernacle is conceived as God's new "creation."

The instructions for building the furniture and furnishings of the Tabernacle in 25:1–30:10 may be outlined in a nested menorah pattern:

Tabernacle Furniture and Furnishings   *Exod 25:1–30:10*

A	Ark of the Covenant	25:10–22
B	Table for the bread of the Presence	25:23–30
C	The golden menorah (lampstand)	25:31–40
X	**Instructions for building the Meeting Tent**	26:1–37
C´	Altar for burnt offering	27:1–8
B´	Court of the Tabernacle and instructions for ordaining the priests	27:9–29:46
A´	Golden altar for burning incense—before the veil	30:1–10

2nd Level Menorah: Instructions for Building the Meeting Tent   *Exodus 26*

A	Tapestry covering of fine linen—ten panels with 50 loops and 50 clasps	26:1–6
B	Tapestry covering of goats' hair—eleven panels	26:7–10
C	Bronze clasps (50)	26:11–14
X	**Upright frames [20 + 6 + 20 = 46]**	26:15–25
C´	Horizontal "bars" (to tie the framework together) [5 + 5 + 5 = 15]	26:26–30
B´	The veil (separating the Holy Place from the Holy of Holies)	26:31–35
A´	The Screen (at the entrance to the Meeting Tent)	26:36–37

The concentric structure converges first on the instructions for building the Meeting Tent in Exodus 26. Within that chapter, the focus narrows to the instructions for building the upright frames on which the two tapestry coverings are placed to construct the sanctuary. It is interesting to note that the sanctuary contains a total of 46 (= 2 x 23) of these frames in a pattern of twenty on each side and six on the western wall of the sanctuary. The numerical value of the word "glory" (spelled כבוד) is 23. As one moves from the entrance of the Holy Place to the far wall of the Holy of Holies, there are 20 + 6 = 26 upright frames, numbering from either side, to reach the farthest extent of the Holy of Holies. Since the number 26 is the numerical value of the divine name Yahweh (יהוה), this is a symbolic way of saying that the glory and presence of Yahweh is found in the Meeting Tent.

In terms of literary structure, the account of the construction of the Tabernacle is quite different from the instructions given earlier. The content of Exodus 35–40 can be outlined in a menorah pattern, as follows:

The Construction and Erection of the Tabernacle — Exod 35:1–40:15

A	Yahweh commands the people (through Moses) to keep the Sabbath	35:1–3
B	Moses instructs the people to take an offering for building the Tabernacle	35:4–29
C	Moses said: Yahweh has called Bezalel and Oholiab	35:30–35
X	**Bezalel and Oholiab shall do what Yahweh has commanded**	36:1
C´	Moses called Bezalel and Oholiab and they received the offering	36:2–5
B´	Moses commands the people to refrain from giving more	36:6–39:43
A´	Yahweh commands Moses to erect and furnish the Tabernacle	40:1–15

Unlike the instructions given in Exodus 25–30, which focus on the building of the Meeting Tent and its structural framework in particular, the focus of attention here is on Bezalel and Oholiab, the craftsmen Yahweh selected to do the work. The construction of the Tabernacle is developed in another menorah pattern, which is framed by parallel references to Bezalel and Oholiab.

Construction of the Tabernacle by Bezalel and Oholiab — Exod 36:2–38:20

A	Bezalel and Oholiab receive the offerings for the work	36:2–7
B	They make the linen tapestry covering with loops and clasps	36:8–13
C	They make the goats' hair tapestry covering with loops and clasps	36:14–19
X	**They make the upright frames [20 + 6 + 20 = 46]**	36:20–30
C´	They make the horizontal "bars" (to tie the framework together)	36:31–34
B´	They make the veil, screen and five pillars for the Meeting Tent	36:35–38
A´	Bezalel and Oholiab make the furniture for the Tabernacle	37:1–38:20

Like the parallel discussion in Exodus 25–30, the focus of attention here is on the construction of the framework of the Meeting Tent, with its focus on the two sacred numbers, 23 and 26. The Tabernacle is intended to house the glory of Yahweh's presence in the midst of the people of Israel.

The concluding section of Exodus, which explores the role of Moses who erects the completed Tabernacle, may be outlined in a somewhat different manner:

Moses Finishes the Work—the Tabernacle is Erected — 40:16–33

a	The tabernacle complex is erected on the 1st day of the 1st month	40:16–17
A	Moses sets up bases, frames, poles, pillars and tapestry coverings	40:18–19
B	The Ark of the Covenant is screened off with its contents	40:20–21
C	Moses puts the table in the Meeting Tent with bread in order	40:22–23
X	**Moses puts the menorah in the Meeting Tent**	40:24–25
C´	Moses sets up the golden incense altar and burns incense on it	40:26–27
B´	Moses sets up the screen for the tent and altar of burnt offering	40:28–29
A´	Moses sets up the laver between the tent and the altar	40:30–32
a´	Moses erects the court and the screen at the entrance gate	40:33

The repeated phrase, "as Yahweh had commanded Moses," appears seven times (vv 19, 21, 23, 25, 27, 29, and 32—marking the sections of a menorah pattern. A framework is placed around this menorah pattern. In 40:16 Moses did "according to all that Yahweh commanded him, so he did." In 40:33, the section concludes with the words, "So Moses finished the work." As we will see in chapter 3, that work includes another way of looking at the Tabernacle—in the literary structure of the book of Leviticus.

Concept Check #11

Why is it important for followers of Yeshua today to learn about the use of the Tabernacle in the religion of ancient Israel?

Check your answer at the back of this book.

E. Passover within the Canonical Process

The original Passover feast is described in Exod 12:1–28. On the tenth day of the first month (Nisan), the people of Israel "are to take a lamb for each family, a lamb for each household" (12:3). The lamb is to "be without blemish, a year-old male; you make take it from the sheep or from the goats" (12:5). It is to be kept until the fourteenth day of the month, and then slaughtered at twilight (12:6). Its blood is to be placed "on the two doorposts and the lintel of the houses in which they eat it" (12:7). It is to be eaten—"You shall let none of it remain until the morning; anything that remains until the morning you shall burn" (12:10). During that night, Yahweh himself passed through the land of Egypt and struck down every first-born in the land of Egypt, both human beings and animals. The blood on the houses was a sign. Yahweh passed over those houses.

The death of the first-born in Egypt was the tenth and final plague, after which the people of Israel left Egypt and slavery. They crossed *Yam Suf* (Sea of Reeds) and made their way through the wilderness to Mount Sinai. The second observance of Passover within the biblical record took place a year later at Mount Sinai (Num 9:1–15), just before the people began their journey northward to the Promised Land. But they did not make it; and thirty-nine years passed before the text records another observance of Passover, which took place at Gilgal immediately after Joshua and the people of Israel "passed over" the Jordan River and established camp near Jericho—the third Passover of biblical tradition (Josh 5:10–12).

The fourth recorded observance of Passover within the Torah and the Former Prophets took place in Jerusalem in the time of King Josiah (2 Kings 23). "No such Passover had been kept since the days of the judges who judged Israel, or during all the days of the kings of Israel or of the kings of Judah" (2 Kings 23:22).

The fifth Passover within the Torah and the Prophets is described briefly in Ezek 45:21–25, in which the prophet anticipates a future celebration in the rebuilt Temple in Jerusalem. Two more observances of Passover appear in the Writings: that of Hezekiah (2 Chronicles 30) and Ezra (Ezra 6). The seven observances of Passover within the Tanakh may be outlined in a menorah pattern, as follows:

The Seven Passovers in the Tanakh   *Exodus–Ezra*

A   Original Passover in Egypt—before crossing *Yam Suf* (Sea of Reeds)   Exod 12–15
B   Passover at Mount Sinai—a year later   Num 9:1–15
C   Joshua's Passover at Gilgal—after crossing the Jordan River   Josh 5:10–12
X   **Hezekiah's Passover in Jerusalem—anticipating the future**   2 Chronicles 30
C´ Josiah's Passover in Jerusalem [see 2 Chronicles 35]   2 Kings 23:21–23
B´ Ezekiel's future Passover—anticipated in the new Temple   Ezek 45:21–25
A´ Ezra's Passover—at the rebuilt Temple in Jerusalem   Ezra 6:19–22

In this reading, the celebrations of the Festival of Passover on the part of Joshua and Josiah function as an envelope to frame both the Former Prophets as a literary unit and the insertion of the Passover of Hezekiah recorded in 2 Chronicles. Hezekiah invited all Israel and Judah, including the tribes of Ephraim and Manasseh, to come to the Temple in Jerusalem to observe the Passover in the second month (2 Chron 30:1–2). The time was changed to accommodate the priests who "had not sanctified themselves in sufficient number, nor had the people assembled in Jerusalem" (30:3). But the people in the northern parts of Israel "laughed them to scorn and mocked them. Only a few from Asher, Manasseh and Zebulun humbled themselves and came to Jerusalem" to celebrate Passover (30:10–11).

The pairing of Moses and Ezra here is apropos. Moses wrote the Torah, and Ezra brought it to Jerusalem. In Jewish tradition, Ezra is considered to be second only to Moses in importance, and both are closely connected with the Torah. Ezra read the Torah to the people on the first day of the seventh month—reading "from early morning until midday, in the presence of the men and the women and those who could understand; and the ears of all the people were attentiave to the (reading from the) scroll of the Torah" (Neh 8:3). "Ezra opened the scroll in the sight of all the people . . . So they read from the scroll, from the Torah of God, with interpretation. They gave the sense, so that the people understood the reading" (Neh 8:5–8).

The pairing of Joshua and Josiah in this structure foreshadows the Passover of another "Joshua" in the distant future—this time in Jerusalem. That same Passover is the focus of Ezekiel's brief provision for the celebration of Passover within the context of the Second Temple in Jerusalem and that of Ezra as well. In the structure presented here, Ezra's Passover is linked with the original observance of Passover in Egypt (Exodus 12–13). It's meaning is foreshadowed in the mystery of the *Akedah* (the "binding" of Isaac) in Genesis 22.

Passover took on a radical new interpretation as observed by Yeshua with his disciples shortly before his crucifixion. As Yeshua put it, "I have eagerly desired to eat this Passover with you before I suffer; for I tell you, I will not eat it until it is fulfilled in the kingdom of God" (Luke 22:15). At this point, he took the bread and the cup in the Passover meal and transformed them into what Christians call the Eucharist. Moreover, the passion event itself became a symbolic Passover, in which the life and death of Jesus is read through the lens of the Passover tradition. As the apostle Paul put it, "For Christ, our paschal lamb, has been sacrificed. Let us, therefore, celebrate the festival . . . with the unleavened bread of sincerity and truth" (1 Cor 5:7–8).

The Pentateuchal Structure of the Book of Exodus

[Four Wheels of the Same Likeness and a Wheel within the Four Wheels]

A	*Moses Delivers Israel from Slavery in Egypt*	*Exod 1:1–15:19*
a	Call and naming of Moses	1:1–4:31
b	Contest with Pharaoh—climaxed with death of the first-born	5:1–11:10
x	**Institution of the Passover**	12:1–51
b´	Consecration of the first-born	13:1–22
a´	Crossing of *Yam Suf* (Sea of Reeds)	14:1–15:19
B	*Journey to Mount Sinai—Manna in the Wilderness*	*Exod 15:10–18:27*
a	Miriam's song	15:20–21
b	Crisis in the wilderness—bitter water made sweet (Marah)	15:22–27
x	**Bread for the wilderness-Manna**	16:1–36
b´	Crises in the wilderness—water from the rock (Massah and Meribah)	17:1–16
a´	Jethro's visit	18:1–27
X	*Theophany at Sinai: God Reveals Himself*	*Exodus 19–24*
a	Theophany at Sinai: Moses receives the commandments	19:1–25
b	Ten Commandments given	20:1–17
x	**Theophany at Sinai: Moses meets God in thick darkness**	20:18–21
b´	Book of the Covenant	20:22–23:33
a´	Theophany and covenant ceremony—Moses with priests	24:1–18
B´	*Life at Sinai: The Building of the Tabernacle*	*Exodus 25–39*
a	Tabernacle designed	25:1–31:18
b	The covenant broken—Golden Calf incident	32:1–35
x	**Yahweh's guiding presence revealed**	33:1–23
b´	The covenant renewed	34:1–35
a´	Tabernacle constructed	35:1–39:42
A´	*The Glory of Yahweh Fills the Tabernacle*	*Exodus 40*
a	Moses blesses the people for completing the work	39:43
b	Yahweh instructs Moses to erect the Tabernacle	40:1–11
x	**Aaron and sons chosen to be a perpetual priesthood**	40:12–15
b´	Moses erects the Tabernacle: "So Moses finished the work"	40:16–33
a´	The glory of Yahweh fills the Tabernacle	40:34–38

Study Questions

These study questions are optional and are designed for the student who wishes to go beyond what is required. *Do not send them to the Center for evaluation.*

1. What do you think were some life changing events for Moses? How do you think he was changed?

2. What is the significance of the ten plagues?

3. What is the significance of each piece of furniture in the Tabernacle?

4. What are some of the important truths that Exodus teaches about God? About human beings? Are these truths applicable today?

5. How would you describe the conversations between Moses and God in the book of Exodus? What lessons about prayer and fellowship with God can be learned from this?

6. What truths about Yeshua the Messiah (Jesus Christ) and his ministry are foreshadowed in Exodus? Spend much time thinking about this.

7. What lessons about leadership may be learned from the example of Moses?

8. What does Exodus teach about obedience?

9. How do you define *worship*? What truths about worship does Exodus teach?

3

The Book of Leviticus

Contents

A. Yahweh's Hidden Presence in Leviticus and the Torah
B. The Tabernacle in the Book of Leviticus
C. Reading the Book of Leviticus from the Center
D. Holiness in the Book of Leviticus
E. Exodus and Leviticus as a Literary Unit

Objectives

When this chapter is completed, the student should be able to:

♦ List and briefly describe the offerings presented to God in Leviticus 1–7
♦ Discuss the meaning of the term "leprosy" as used in the book of Leviticus
♦ Discuss the structure of the book of Leviticus as a projection of the architectural design of the Tabernacle
♦ Discuss the meaning of holiness
♦ Explain the importance of the Day of Atonement in ancient Israel

A. Yahweh's Hidden Presence in Leviticus and the Torah

In Jewish tradition, the name of the third book of the Torah is ויקרא (pronounced *Va-yikra'*), the first word in the Hebrew text, which is translated, "And he proclaimed (from the Meeting Tent)." What Yahweh proclaimed to Moses is essentially a handbook on holiness; for the word "holy" (or one of its derivatives) appears eighty-seven times in twenty-seven chapters. In early rabbinical times, the book was called *Torat Kohanim*, "the priest's manual." The name Leviticus is derived from the Septuagint—the Levitical book, the book that deals mainly with the Levitical priests and their duties.

As the third book in the Torah, Leviticus is the structural center of the five books of Moses. The opening verse of the book of Leviticus is made up of nine words in the Hebrew text, in which the middle word is the divine name Yahweh (יהוה). Moreover, the name "YHWH" is spelled out in fixed intervals with the letters יהוה being seven letters apart. Starting with the י of the first word ויקרא, "and he summoned," count seven letters and the next one is ה in the word משה, "Moses." Count seven more letters and the next one is ו in the word יהוה, "YHWH." Count seven letters again and the next one is ה in the word מאהל,

"from the tent." The sequence spells out the name יהוה, which is indeed a fitting word to find in the structural center of the introductory words of the central book in the Torah.

A close look at the opening verses of the other four books in the Torah reveals that the phenomenon in Leviticus is not a coincidence. In Gen 1:1–5, we find the word תורה, "Torah," spelled out in fixed intervals 49 letters apart. Starting with the final letter of the first word in the Bible, בראשית, "in the beginning," which is ת, we count 49 letters and the next one is ו in the word תהום, "the deep." Count 49 letters again and the next one is ר in the word וירא, "and he saw." And, finally, count 49 letters once again and the next one is ה in the word אלהים, "God." The sequence spells out the word תורה, "Torah."

The same phenomenon appears in Exod 1:1–6. Here the ת is the final letter of the second word in the opening phrase ואלה שמות, "and these are the names [of the children of Israel]." It should be noted in passing that for both Genesis and Exodus the sequence begins with the final letter in what is taken as the title of these books in Jewish tradition. Count 49 letters once again and the next letter is ו in the word ויהודה, "and Judah." Count 49 letters again and the next one is ר in the word ירך, "loins (of Jacob)." Finally, count 49 letters once again and the next one is ה in the word ההוא, "that (generation)." The sequence spells out the word תורה, "Torah."

In the book of Numbers the situation shifts. The word תורה, "Torah," is spelled in reverse beginning with the first occurrence of ה at the end of the word משה, "Moses." Count 49 letters and the next letter is ר in the word מצרים, "Egypt." Count 49 letters and the next letter is ו in the word שמות. Count 49 letters again and the next letter is ת in the word אתם, "them."

In the book of Deuteronomy the situation shifts once again. This time the sequence begins with the first occurrence of the word תורה, "Torah," in 1:5. As in the introduction to Numbers, the word תורה, "Torah," is spelled in reverse between a fixed sequence of letters. For some reason, however, the number of letters between each of the four consonants is one less than the forty-nine used in the books of Genesis, Exodus, and Numbers. After the first letter of the word התורה, "the Torah," count 48 letters and the next one is the letter ר in the word בהר, "in the mountain." Count 48 letters again and the next one is ו in the word ובנגב, "and in the Negev" (1:7). Count 48 letters again and the next one is the first of two consecutive occurrences of ת in the word נתתי, "I have given."

One can imagine the effort it took on the part of scribes in antiquity to arrange the Hebrew text at the beginning of each of the five books of Moses to encode this information at fixed intervals in the sequence of consonants. It is interesting to note the particular words that were selected in the five books in question to achieve this phenomenon. When these words are arranged consecutively, along with the words that make up the traditional titles of each of the five books of Moses, they may be read as a hidden message that makes good sense:

> In the beginning there was a primeval ocean and God appeared.
> And these are *the names*—
> And Judah is the loins (base of the menorah) [see Exod 25:31; 37:17; Num 8:4]
> And Yahweh summoned Moses and spoke to him from the Meeting Tent.
> Yahweh spoke to Moses in the wilderness of Egypt *their names*—

These are the words of the Torah,
which I have given you on the mountain and in the Negev.

The two occurrences of the word שמות, "names," in this hidden message call attention to the names of the "children of Israel" and probably to the ineffable name, Yahweh, as well—particularly in terms of the divine-name numbers 26 and 17. These two numbers are coded into the Hebrew text of the Torah in many different ways.[1] It was memory of this phenomenon that led medieval Jewish mystics to note that the divine name was woven into the very fabric of the Hebrew text of the Bible. Here the divine name יהוה, "YHWH," appears precisely in the center of this structure as the central word in Lev 1:1, where the divine name is spelled out in a fixed sequence in which each letter is separated from the next by seven other letters. Another hidden message may be to look for the number seven—i.e., the menorah pattern, as a key to finding the literary structure of the Torah.

Concept Check #12

How much time elapsed between the completion of the Tabernacle in Exod 40:33 and the departure of the people of Israel from Mount Sinai in Num 10:11?

Check your answer at the back of this book.

B. The Tabernacle in the Book of Leviticus

According to the anthropologist Mary Douglas, the governing principle in the organization of Leviticus as a whole is the architectural design of the Tabernacle.[2]

The entrance to the Tabernacle complex opens to a large outer court measuring fifty by fifty cubits, which has near its center the large altar for sacrificial offerings and the laver used by the priests to wash themselves. A screen separates the Tabernacle from the outer court. Beyond the screen are two rooms, the first of which is the Holy Place measuring twenty by ten cubits that contains the lampstand, the table for the bread of the presence, and the altar of incense. A second screen separates this room from the Holy of Holies, which measures 2½ by 2½ cubits. The ark is located beneath the shadowing protective wings of two cherubim. The content of the twenty-seven chapters of Leviticus is projected on this grand plan of the Tabernacle, as shown in the drawing at the bottom of the following page.

Reading Leviticus in terms of the architectural design of the Tabernacle suggests that the function of the book is to bring us into the Holy Place to encounter God. To bridge the gap between finite and sinful human beings and an infinite and holy God, three things are required:

---

1   See Casper J. Labuschagne, *Numerical Secrets of the Bible: Rediscovering the Bible Codes* (Richland Hills, TX: BIBAL Press, 2000).

2   Mary Douglas, *Leviticus as Literature* (Oxford University Press, 1999).

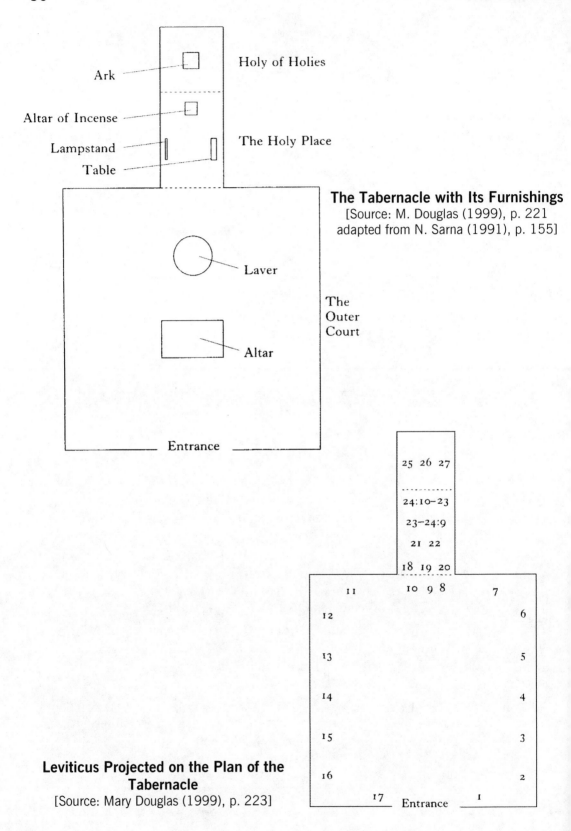

Ark

Altar of Incense

Lampstand

Table

Holy of Holies

The Holy Place

The Tabernacle with Its Furnishings
[Source: M. Douglas (1999), p. 221
adapted from N. Sarna (1991), p. 155]

Laver

The
Outer
Court

Altar

Entrance

25 26 27

24:10–23

23–24:9

21 22

18 19 20

11   10 9 8   7

12   6

13   5

14   4

15   3

**Leviticus Projected on the Plan of the
Tabernacle**
[Source: Mary Douglas (1999), p. 223]

16   2

17   Entrance   1

1. we must bring sacrificial offerings Leviticus 1–7
2. we need a priest to mediate in our behalf   Leviticus 8–10
3. expiatory process must eliminate impurity at all levels Leviticus 11–17

The first seven chapters of Leviticus take the reader from the entrance of the Tabernacle to the first of two narrative screens (10:1–7 and 24:10–23). The sacrificial offerings of Leviticus 1–7 are offered on the altar for burnt offerings in the outer court. The first screen of the Tabernacle includes the fire narrative in which Nadab and Abihu, the sons of Aaron, are consumed by Yahweh's fire (10:1–2). The way of purification continues in the outer court of the Tabernacle (chaps. 11–16), as worshipers make their way symbolically back to the entrance of the Tabernacle. The ritual of the Day of Atonement provides the purification of the sanctuary itself (chap. 16), which enables the worshiper to pass through the screen from the outer court to the Holy Place (chaps. 17–24). Here we find the central chapter of the book, with its instructions for the life of moral and ritual holiness (chap. 19). Holiness in daily life is explored further in chaps. 20–24, which reach their climax in the stoning narrative of 24:10–23. This episode of punishment for blasphemy (violation of the 3rd Commandment) constitutes the second screen, which separates the Holy Place (chaps. 17–24) from the Holy of Holies (chaps. 25–27). Within the Holy of Holies we find the covenant stipulations, including the blessings and curses (chap. 26). On either side of this pivotal chapter, we find proclamations of liberty—in person-to-person obligations (25:2–55) and in debts to Yahweh (with religious vows, 27:1–33).

Concept Check #13

How does the content of the book of Leviticus differ from that of the other two wilderness books on either side of it?

Check your answer at the back of this book.

C. Reading the Book of Leviticus from the Center

1. The Ten Parashoth in the Book of Leviticus

Jewish tradition divides Leviticus into ten Parashoth (weekly portions), which appear to be structured in five major parts, as follows:

The Ten Parashoth in Leviticus	*Parashoth*	*Lev 1–27*
A Sacrificial instructions directed to the laity	1:1–6:7	Parashah 24
B Sacrifices with priestly tasks and prerogatives	6:8–8:36	Parashah 25
X 1st screen—**denying entrance to the Holy Place**	9:1–11:47	Parashah 26
B´ Removing impurity so as to enter the Holy Place	12:1–18:30	Parashoth 27–29
A´ Going from the Holy Place to the Holy of Holies	19:1–27:34	Parashoth 30–33

Each of these five sections of the book of Leviticus may be outlined in a menorah pattern or a nested series of menorah patterns.

2. Sacrificial Instruction Directed to the Laity (Lev 1:1–6:7)

Parashah 24: Va-yikra' (He called)	*Lev 1:1–6:7*
A The burnt offering—a sacrifice of praise; completely burned	1:1–17
B The cereal offering—unburned portion is consumed by the priests	2:1–16
C The well-being (peace) offering—a covenant meal	3:1–16
X **Warning: "you may eat neither suet (fat) nor blood"**	3:17
C´ The purification (sin) offering—efficacious only for unwitting sin	4:1–35
B´ The graduated purification (sin) offering—so that all may participate	5:1–13
A´ The reparation (guilt) offering—for offenses requiring restitution	5:14–6:7

Since the suet (fat) and the blood of sacrificial animals belongs to Yahweh, it must be consumed by fire on the altar. With this principle in the center, five types of offerings are delineated. On one side, the offerings progress from those that are consumed in their entirety on the altar (burnt offerings, chap. 1), to those that are consumed by the priests alone (cereal offerings, chap. 2), to those consumed by the entire worshiping community in a covenant meal ("peace" offerings, chap. 3). On the other side, we find a progression of offerings designed to deal with impurity caused by unwitting sins. There is no prescribed offering to deal with deliberate disobedience by violating the stipulations of the covenant agreement; for sacrifice is not a magical means of atonement. It is an act of worship.

3. Sacrifices with priestly tasks and prerogatives (Lev 6:8–8:36)

The second of the weekly portions (Parashah 25), which concerns the same offerings from the perspective of priestly instructions and elaboration of priestly prerogatives, may be outlined in a menorah pattern, as follows:

Parashah 25: Tsav (Give an order)	*Lev 6:8–8:36*
A Burnt offering—a perpetual fire shall be kept burning on the altar	6:8–13
B Cereal offering and the high priests daily cereal offering	6:14–23
C Purification (sin) offering—eaten by priests	6:24–29
X **Warning: offerings on the Day of Atonement cannot be eaten**	6:30
C´ Reparation (guilt) offering and priestly dues from the holy offerings	7:1–10
B´ Well-being (peace) offering and the priestly dues from them	7:11–37
A´ Consecration of the priests—in the matter of ordination sacrifices	8:1–36

In the structural center of this menorah pattern we find a warning. Any offering from which blood is brought into the Meeting Tent to make atonement in the Holy Place cannot be eaten—"it shall be burned with fire" (6:30).

The concluding section in the above menorah pattern, which deals with priestly ordination, may be explored in another menorah pattern:

The Ordination of the Priests   *Leviticus 8*

A   The congregation is assembled at the door of the Meeting Tent   8:1–9
B   The ceremony of anointment—the Tabernacle, its altar, and Aaron   8:10–13
C   Offering the bull of the sin offering for the priests   8:14–17
X   **Offering the ram of the burnt offering**   8:18–21
C´   Offering the ram of ordination   8:22–29
B´   The priests and their garments are consecrated with anointing oil   8:30
A´ Aaron and his sons serve at the door of the Meeting Tent seven days   8:31–36

This ceremony of ordination fulfills what Moses was commanded to do in Exod 29:4–6. In preparation for this ceremony, the entire congregation assembles at the door of the Meeting Tent (8:1–9). At the conclusion of the ceremony, Aaron and his sons take their place at the door of the Meeting Tent. They boil the meat of the sacrificial offering "at the door of the Meeting Tent, and there eat it and the bread that is in the basket of ordination offerings" (8:31, RSV). Aaron and his sons remain at the door of the Meeting Tent for seven days performing what Yahweh commanded through Moses (8:36). The structural center of this literary unit focuses on "the ram of the burnt offering," which enables Aaron and his sons to perform their duties in behalf of the congregation in holiness.

4. Priestly Ordination and Divine Judgment (Leviticus 9–11)

The service of ordination in Leviticus 8 sets the stage for the commencement of Aaron's high priesthood:

Parashah 26: Shemini (Eighth)   *Leviticus 9–11*

A   Commencement of Aaron's high priesthood: sin offering and burnt offering   9:1–14
B   Aaron presents the people's offerings (as instructed in chaps. 1–7)   9:15–21
C   Aaron blesses the people and Yahweh's fire consumes the offering   9:22–24
X   **Nadab and Abihu are consumed by Yahweh's fire**   10:1–7
C´   Yahweh commands Aaron to be holy when entering the Tabernacle   10:8–11
B´ Aaron defends Eleazar and Ithamar for not eating the priestly portions   10:12–20
A´ Diet laws (+ addendum: priests must decide what is clean and unclean)   11:1–47

The focus of attention here is on what Mary Douglas calls the first of two narrative screens that correspond to the curtains at the entrance to the Holy Place and the Holy of Holies. In Jewish tradition, Parashah 26 is called *Shemini* ("Eight")—a reference to the eighth day, following the seven-day ordination ceremony (8:33). On that day something mysterious happened. Two of Aaron's sons, Nadab and Abihu, offered unauthorized fire before Yahweh—"And fire came forth from the presence of Yahweh and devoured them, and they died before Yahweh" (10:2). The passage displays the familiar qualities of the "riddle in the middle" in that the biblical text does not specify precisely what their sin was in presenting this "unholy fire." At any rate, as Mary Douglas observes, the progression of movement into the Meeting Tent symbolically is interrupted sharply by this brief narrative. Readers must remain in the outer court of the Tabernacle and make their way back to its entrance once again. While doing so, they must purge themselves of all impurity. Only then can their high priest take them inside the Holy Place where they will find the path to ritual and moral holiness in Leviticus 19. The rich symbolism here takes on deeper meaning in relation to Yeshua the Messiah (Jesus Christ) in Hebrew 9:11–10:18.

5. Removing Impurity in order to Enter the Holy Place (Leviticus 12–18)

The task of purgation in route to holiness is explored in another menorah pattern that includes three weekly portions in the annual cycle of readings from the Torah (Parashoth 27–29). These seven chapters of Leviticus, which take the reader back to the door of the Meeting Tent and from there into the Holy Place, may be outlined in a nested menorah pattern, as follows:

Parashoth 27–29 in a Menorah Pattern	*Leviticus 12–18*
A Purification of a woman after childbirth	12:1–8
B "Leprosy" and Purification after "leprosy"	13:1–14:57
C Purification in the loss of vital fluids—male and female	15:1–33
X **The Day of Atonement**	16:1–34
C´ The slaughter and consumption of meat	17:1–16
B´ As a holy people, Israel must not follow pagan practices	18:1–5
A´ Illicit sexual practices	18:6–30

2nd Level Menorah: The Day of Atonement	*Leviticus 16*
A Setting: Yahweh speaks to Moses after the death of Nadab and Abihu	16:1
B Precautions and provisions—putting on vestments and ritual washing	16:2–5
C Purgation ritual—Aaron offers a bull and a goat as sin offerings	16:6–19
X **The scapegoat ritual—2nd goat released in "a solitary land"**	16:20–22a
C´ The altar sacrifices—Aaron offers burnt offerings	16:22b–25
B´ Purification of the high priest's assistants	16:26–28
A´ The date is fixed for all time—the 10th day of the 7th month	16:29–34

The structure of the nested menorah pattern here moves from the death of Nadab and Abihu (10:1–7), in the center of the previous menorah pattern, to the institution of the Day of Atonement (chap. 16), which begins with a specific reference to that earlier event (16:1). The nested concentric structure converges on the scapegoat ritual, in which Aaron imparts the sin of the people to a goat, which is released in the wilderness (16:20–22a). The outermost frame concerns purification in sexual matters (12:1–8 and 18:6–30). The second frame presents a lengthy section on "leprosy" and its purification (chaps. 13–14), which is set over against a much shorter passage that enjoins Israel to be a holy people by not following pagan practices (18:1–5). The third frame opens with a chapter on purification from contamination from bodily discharges (chap. 15), and continues with another chapter on contamination from improperly prepared foods into the body (chap. 17). Between these two chapters stands the account of the Day of Atonement, which is explored in a second-level menorah pattern.

　　Within the above menorah pattern, Leviticus 15 displays a menorah pattern of its own, as the following outline of its contents shows:

Purification in the Loss of Vital Fluids—Male and Female   *Leviticus 15*

A	Yahweh tells Moses and Aaron to instruct the people of Israel	15:1–2a
B	Abnormal male discharges	15:2b–15
C	Normal male discharges	15:16–17
X	**Marital intercourse**	15:18
C´	Normal female discharges	15:19–24
B´	Abnormal female discharges	15:25–30
A´	Consequences for the sanctuary and for the people of Israel	15:31–33

Both contaminating and normal bodily discharges of the two sexes are carefully arranged in a concentric pattern, with a single verse on the union of the two sexes in the center.

6. Going from the Holy Place to the Holy of Holies (Leviticus 19–27)

In the concluding four weekly portions in Leviticus (Parashoth 30–33), we find a nested menorah pattern that highlights the central teaching of the book:

Parashoth 30–33 in a Menorah Pattern   *Leviticus 19–27*

A	Inside the Holy Place—ritual and moral holiness	19:1–37
B	Penalties for Molek worship, necromancy and sexual offences	20:1–27
C	Restrictions placed on priests to guard against ritual defilement	21:1–22:33
X	**The holiness calendar**	23:1–44
C´	Oil for the lampstand and bread for the Table of Presence	24:1–9
B´	The case of blasphemy—2nd narrative screen	24:10–23
A´	Inside the Holy of Holies: Liberation in the covenant relationship	25:1–27:34

2nd Level Menorah: The Holiness Calendar   *Leviticus 23*

A	Yahweh instructs Moses on the appointed feasts	23:1–2
B	Sabbath—the 7th day is a Sabbath of solemn rest	23:3
C	Summary: "These are the appointed feasts of Yahweh"	23:4
X	**Spring and fall festivals—leave gleanings for the poor**	23:5–36
C´	Summary: "These are the appointed feasts of Yahweh"	23:37–38
B´	Sukkot—"You shall dwell in booths for seven days" [15 Tishri]	23:39–43
A´	Moses instructs the people on the appointed feasts	23:44

3rd Level Menorah: Spring and Fall Festivals—Leave Gleanings   *Lev 23:5–36*

A	Festival of Passover and Unleavened Bread [14–15 Nisan]	23:5–8
B	Wave offering [day after last Sabbath of Unleavened Bread]	23:9–14
C	Festival of Weeks (Pentecost)—50 days after wave offering	23:15–21
X	**Leave gleanings for the poor when you reap the harvest**	23:22
C´	Festival of trumpets (New Year) [1 Tishri]	23:23–25
B´	Day of Atonement—"a sabbath of solemn rest" [10 Tishri]	23:26–32
A´	Festival of Booths—seven day festival [15–22 Tishri]	23:33–36

The outer frame here opens with a chapter on ritual and moral holiness (Leviticus 19), which Mary Douglas describes as the central chapter of Leviticus. From an architectural point of view, this is the goal worshipers are seeking as they move from the outer court of the Tabernacle into the Holy Place within the Meeting Tent. That chapter is set over against the concluding three chapters (Leviticus 25–27), which correspond to the Holy of Holies. The second narrative screen in 24:10–23 forms the barrier between these two places.

The last two weekly portions (Parashoth 32–33) in Leviticus may also be outlined in a menorah pattern:

Parashoth 32–33: Liberation in the Covenant Relationship	*Leviticus 25–27*
A Sinai opening: "Yahweh spoke to Moses *on Mount Sinai*, saying"	25:1
B The sabbatical year—"of solemn rest for the land"	25:2–7
C Proclamation of liberty in person-to-person obligations (Jubilee)	25:8–55
X **Covenant stipulations with blessings and curses *on Mount Sinai***	26:1–46
C´ Proclamation of liberty in debts to Yahweh (with religious vows)	27:1–29
B´ The tithe is holy to Yahweh, it shall not be redeemed	27:30–33
A´ Sinai ending: "the commandments Yahweh gave *on Mount Sinai*"	27:34

The beginning, middle, and end of this concentric unit are marked by repetition of the phrase "on Mount Sinai," as Mary Douglas has noted. The second frame moves from a brief section on the sabbatical year in Israel (32:2–5), to another on the holiness of the tithe (27:30–33). The innermost frame focuses on the theme of liberty. On the one hand, it is liberty in person-to-person obligations in terms of the year of Jubilee (25:8–55). On the other, it is liberty in relation to obligations owed to Yahweh himself in terms of religious vows (27:1–29). The center of this concluding section focuses on the blessings and the curses of the covenant God has established with his people (Leviticus 26).

Concept Check #14

What has replaced the sacrificial system in Jewish worship since the destruction of the Temple in Jerusalem?

Check your answer at the back of this book.

D. Holiness in the Book of Leviticus

The classic treatment of the term "holy" is that of Rudolf Otto in his book, *The Idea of the Holy* (New York: Oxford University Press, 1958; c1923). He starts with a discussion of the concept of the "numinous," and then introduces the Latin words *mysterium tremendum*, which he explores at length. In the simplest terms, holiness is different from the ordinary or profane. It is something "other." The "holy" is powerful or numinous. The presence of the holy inspires awe. The holy may be perceived as dangerous; but at the same time it evokes deep fascination—it is desired because it affords blessing, power, and protection.

The book of Leviticus is a treatise on holiness within the context of a specific society in the ancient Near East. The key chapter on holiness is Leviticus 19, which begins with the injunction, "You shall be holy, for I Yahweh your God am holy" (19:2). This means that the people of Israel, in becoming a holy nation, must preserve their distinctiveness from other peoples. They must pursue a way of life that is different from that practiced by their neighbors. Their calling is summarized in Exod 19:6—"you shall be to me a kingdom of priests and a holy nation." This statement suggests, as Baruch Levine has noted, that "holiness cannot be achieved by individuals alone, no matter how elevated, pure, or righteous. It can be realized only through the life of the community, acting together."[3]

When the book of Leviticus is outlined in a nested menorah pattern, the focus of attention is on holiness:

The Book of Leviticus in a Menorah Pattern	*Leviticus 1–27*
A In the outer court—the way to holiness for God's people	1:1–10:20
B In the outer court—the way of purification	11:1–17:16
C Inside the Tabernacle (the Holy Place)—the way of holiness	18:1–30
X **The life of moral and ritual holiness**	19:1–37
C´ Inside the Tabernacle (the Holy Place)—the way of holiness	20:1–22:33
B´ Moving toward the Holy of Holies—holiness in daily life	23:1–24:22
A´ Inside the Holy of Holies: liberation in the covenant relationship	25:1–27:34

2nd Level Menorah: The Life of Moral and Ritual Holiness	*Leviticus 19*
A Keynote: "You shall be holy; for I Yahweh your God am holy"	19:1–2
B Honor your parents, keep the Sabbath and do not turn to idols	19:3–4
C Offer sacrifices as God has instructed or be cut off	19:5–8
X **Ten commandments on living a holy life**	19:9–32
C´ Love your neighbor (i.e., the sojourner) as yourself	19:33–34
B´ Do nothing wrong in your dealings in human society	19:35–36
A´ Summation: "You shall observe all my statutes . . . I am Yahweh"	19:37

As we move more deeply into the structural center of Leviticus in chapter 19, we find an interesting reflection on the Ten Commandments. The outermost frame highlights the central message of the book as a whole, namely a summons to live a life of moral and ritual holiness (19:2 and 19:37). The second frame focuses on four specific commandments in the familiar pattern of three plus one, with modifications of Commandments 1–5 arranged in three parts (19:3–4), which are set over against a summary of Commandments 6–10 (19:35–36). The innermost frame highlights the two primary dimensions in the original Ten Commandments—the vertical dimension in our relationship to God (19:5–8), and the horizontal dimension in our relationship to fellow human beings (19:33–34). And in the structural center we find a listing of specific commandments, which is arranged in ten parts by repetition of the refrain, "I am Yahweh (your God)." These "ten commandments," which constitute the guide to living a holy life, may be summarized as follows:

Ten Commandments for Holy Living in the Book of Leviticus	*Lev 19:9–32*
1. When you harvest the land, leave gleanings for the poor	19:9–10
2. Do not steal, deal falsely, lie, or swear falsely by Yahweh's name	19:11–12
3. Show love to your neighbor, especially those who are handicapped	19:13–14
4. Do no injustice in judgment—show no partiality and do not slander	19:15–16
5. No hatred, vengeance, or grudges—"Love your neighbor as yourself"	19:17–18
6. No illicit mixtures—with livestock, agriculture, and sexual matters	19:19–25

---

3   Baruch Levine, *The JPS Torah Commentary: Leviticus* (Philadelphia: Jewish Publication Society, 1989), p. 256.

7. Do not eat blood, do not participate in the occult and pagan practices   19:26–28
8. No harlotry, keep Yahweh's Sabbaths, reverence God's sanctuary   19:29–30
9. Do not turn to mediums or wizards   19:31
10. Show honor to the elderly and fear God   19:32

Leviticus is much more than a handbook for Levites in ancient Israel to follow in out-
moded ritual practice. Yeshua the Messiah (Jesus Christ) was correct when he concluded
his summary of the demands of the Torah with the simple statement, "You shall love
your neighbor as yourself" (Matt 19:19). He was quoting Lev 19:18, which stands in the
structural center of this list of "ten commandments."

The gulf between the sacred and the profane was not meant to be permanent. The
command to achieve holiness, to become holy, envisions a time when the chasm that separates a holy God from his impure and sinful people is bridged once and for all. That took
place in the great "Day of Atonement"—outside the city of Jerusalem, when the "lamb
of God" was offered as a sacrifice for human sin. We are invited to stand in God's presence as a "holy people"—declared innocent by God himself of our sins, on the basis of
what Yeshua the Messiah (Jesus Christ) accomplished in our behalf. As the apostle Paul
once put it, "he has now reconciled (you) in his body of flesh by his death, in order to present you holy and blameless and irreproachable before him" (Col 1:22).

Concept Check #15

The book of Jonah is included in the afternoon readings for the
Day of Atonement (Yom Kippur) in Judaism. What makes this an
appropriate text?

Check your answer at the back of this book.

E. Exodus and Leviticus as a Literary Unit

The book of Exodus reaches its climax in the building of the Tabernacle, which houses the
presence of Yahweh in all his glory. The book of Leviticus enables the reader to enter that
Tabernacle, at least symbolically. In Leviticus, the narrative story comes to a halt. If Israel is
to be the people of Yahweh, they must take on his character—the way of holiness.

Outlining the two books together in a nested menorah pattern, as follows, demonstrates the fact that Exodus and Leviticus are integrally related:

The Books of Exodus and Leviticus in a Menorah Pattern	*Exodus–Leviticus*
A Naming and call of Moses—God's preparation for his redemptive work	Exod 1:1–3:12
B God reveals his Name to Moses and the contest with Pharaoh	3:13–11:10
C Passover and Festival of Unleavened Bread	12:1–13:16
X **Yahweh's covenant demands holiness**	Exod 13:17–Lev 24:4
C´ Bread for the Table of the Presence in the Tabernacle	Lev 24:5–9
B´ Sin of blaspheming the Name (2nd screen in the Tabernacle)	24:10–23
A´ Inside the Holy of Holies—sabbatical year, jubilee, God's covenant	25:1–27:34

2nd *Level Menorah: The Covenant Demands Holiness* — *Exod 13:17–Lev 24:4*

A   Pillars of cloud and fire—to water from the rock — Exod 13:17–17:7
B   War with Amalek ("holy war") — 17:8–16
C   Sinai revelation—with covenant stipulations — 18:1–23:33
X   **Yahweh's glory poses grave danger** — Exod 24:1–Lev 10:20
C´   Dealing with impurity—Aaron and the Day of Atonement — Lev 11:1–16:34
B´   Inside the Tabernacle—Israel must be holy as God is holy — 17:1–23:44
A´   Oil for the menorah in the Tabernacle — 24:1–4

3rd *Level Menorah: Dangers of Yahweh's Glory* — *Exodus 24–Leviticus 10*

A   Moses brought Aaron, Nadab, Abihu and 70 elders to "see" God — Exod 24:1–14
B   The glory of Yahweh on Mount Sinai — 24:15–18
C   The Tabernacle and its accoutrements designed — 25:1–30:38
X   **Preparations to build the Tabernacle to house Yahweh's glory** — 31:1–36:7
C´   The Tabernacle and its accoutrements constructed — 36:8–40:33
B´   The glory of Yahweh fills the Tabernacle — 40:34–38
A´   Sacrifices and priestly ordination—death of Nadab and Abihu — Lev 1:1–10:20

4th *Level Menorah: Preparations for Building the Tabernacle* — *Exod 31:1–36:7*

A   Bezalel and Oholiab are called to build the Tabernacle — Exod 31:1–11
B   Sabbath law — 31:12–17
C   The two stone tablets of the covenant — 31:18
X   **Covenant broken and renewed at Mount Sinai** — 32:1–34:28
C´   Shining face of Moses [34:29 "with the two tablets"] — 34:29–35
B´   Sabbath regulations — 35:1–3
A´   Offerings to build the Tabernacle given to Bezalel and Oholiab — 35:4–36:7

5th *Level Menorah: Covenant Broken and Renewed at Mount Sinai* — *Exodus 32–34*

A   Covenant broken [Golden Calf incident] — Exod 32:1–35
B   Yahweh speaks: I will not go with this "stiff-necked people" — 33:1–6
C   Moses experienced Yahweh's presence in the Meeting Tent — 33:7–11a
X   **Joshua did not depart from the Meeting Tent** — 33:11b
C´   Moses will experience Yahweh's presence in the future — 33:12–16
B´   Yahweh speaks: I will show you a glimpse of my glory — 33:17–23
A´   Covenant renewed — 34:1–28

This outline of nested menorah patterns suggests that Leviticus was written, together with Exodus 25–40, to form an envelope around the story of the breaking and renewal of the covenant at Mount Sinai (Exodus 32–33).

The Pentateuchal Structure of the Book of Leviticus
[Four Wheels of the Same Likeness and a Wheel within the Four Wheels]

A *The Way to God through the Sacrificial System*	*Leviticus 1–10*
a Offerings that are consumed by fire (in whole or in part)	1:1–3:17
b Offerings in which blood is placed on the horns of the altar	4:1–35
x **Instructions for sacrifice**	5:1–7:38
b´ Rites of ordination in which blood is placed on the horns of the altar	8:1–9:11
a´ Fire consumes priestly offerings (ch 9) and the sons of Aaron (ch 10)	9:12–10:20

B *The Walk with God through the Purity System*	*Leviticus 11–15*
a Clean and unclean foods—what does into the body	11:1–47
b Purification of women after childbirth	12:1–8
x "Leprosy"—varieties and symptoms	13:1–59
b´ Purification of "leprous" persons and houses	14:1–57
a´ Concerning bodily discharges—what comes out of the body	15:1–33

X *The Day of Atonement—the Way to God's Presence*	*Leviticus 16*
a Aaron is to enter the Holy of Holies annually to offer special sacrifices	16:1–3
b Aaron is to put on the holy garments after bathing himself	16:4
x **The purification offerings—a bull and two goats**	16:5–22
b´ Aaron is to take off the holy garments and bathe himself	16:23–28
a´ This annual observance "shall be a statute to you forever"	16:29–34

B´ *The Walk with God through Holiness in Daily Life*	*Leviticus 17–26*
a At the altar: the slaughtering of animals	17:1–16
b Holy people—"You shall be holy" (19:20	18:1–20:27
x **Restrictions placed on priests to guard against ritual defilement**	21:1–22:33
b´ Holy times—"These are the appointed festivals" (23:2)	23:1–24:23
a´ In the land: sabbatical year and year of jubilee and just recompense	25:1–26:46

A´ *The Way to God through Keeping of Holy Vows*	*Leviticus 27*
a Persons dedicated to Yahweh's service may be redeemed	27:1–8
b Only impure animals may be redeemed	27:9–13
x All land is redeemable because land is not offerable	27:14–25
b´ Firstlings must be sacrificed unless defective or impure	27:26–27
a´ Dedications that are "devoted" in holy war may not be redeemed	27:28–34

Study Questions

These study questions are optional and are designed for the student who wishes to go beyond what is required. *Do not send them to the Center for evaluation.*

1. With the five offerings of Leviticus 1–7 in mind, what do you think we should be offering to God today?

2. In what ways does Messiah Yeshua (Jesus Christ) serve as our high priest?

3. What do the chapters about the consecration of the priests teach us about service to God today?

4. What do you consider to be the most important practical teaching of Leviticus for today?

5. What was the purpose of each of the offerings in the book of Leviticus? How did they find their fulfillment in Messiah Yeshua (Jesus Christ)?

6. What was the significance of the Day of Atonement?

7. Do you see any value in the system of encoding hidden information in the opening paragraphs of the five books in the Torah? Why or why not?

The Book of Numbers

Contents

A. The Book of Numbers within the Torah
B. The Wilderness Encampment—Levites as Guards of the Tabernacle
C. Reading the Book of Numbers from the Center
D. Numbers and the "Book of the Wars of Yahweh" (Num 21:14)
E. Numbers within the Primary History—Evidence for a "Master Editor"

Objectives

When this chapter is completed, the student should be able to:

♦ Describe God's provision for Israel in the wilderness

♦ Explain the two phases of the wars of Yahweh as it relates to Moses and Joshua

♦ Explain the significance of the following mountains: Sinai, Hor, and Nebo

♦ Explain the meaning and significance of cities of refuge in ancient Israel

♦ Discuss the major events of Israel's wilderness journey

A. The Book of Numbers within the Torah

In Jewish tradition, the name of the fourth book in the Torah is במדבר (pronounced *bemidbar*, "in the wilderness"), which describes the content of the book better than the title Numbers. The name Numbers is taken from the Septuagint (ancient Greek translation of the Tanakh) from the two numberings of the people in chapters 1 and 26. The book traces what happened to Israel during the forty years they wandered in the wilderness on the edge of the Promised Land. Their journeys take them from Mount Sinai to Kadesh-barnea and eventually to the plains of Moab, where Moses is permitted to see the Promised Land from the top of Mount Nebo before he dies.

The theme of Numbers is the pilgrim journey of God's people on route to the Promised Land—a journey filled with pain and disappointment, as well as hope. Moses faces rebellion on the part of rival leaders, a complaining people, and even national apostasy. Nonetheless, God remains true to his commitment by defeating Israel's enemies, including two Amorite kings in Transjordan (Sihon and Og)—where the tribes of Reuben, Gad, and half of Manasseh settle—and the Midianites who will enter the story again later in the time of Gideon (Judges 6–9).

The forty-year journey through the wilderness from Mount Sinai to Mount Nebo comprises forty-two stations (Numbers 33), which are arranged by "stages according to their starting places" (33:2). The stages fall into three groups:

> ➤ from Rameses (in Egypt, on the day after Passover) to Mount Sinai
> ➤ from Mount Sinai to Mount Hor (where Aaron dies, includes 38 years at Kadesh
> ➤ from Mount Hor to Mount Nebo (where Moses dies, six months after Aaron)

A forty-third stage is implied in the concluding station of the epic journey from Egypt to the Promised Land—the battle camp at Gilgal on the other side of the Jordan River, which Joshua established after Moses' death; for it is there that "the manna ceased" (Josh 5:12). It is interesting to note, in passing, that $43 = 26 + 17$ (the sum of the two divine-name numbers in the composition of the Torah, which are associated with both the name "Yahweh" and the Hebrew word "glory").

The forty years in the wilderness include two generations and the account of each begins with a census (Numbers 1 and 26). The first generation, which is doomed to died in the wilderness for their rebellion (14:32–34), is finally extinguished in the plague at Beth-peor (25:9, 18–19). "Among these there was not one of those enrolled by Moses and Aaron the priest when they recorded the Israelites in the wilderness of Sinai. For Yahweh said to them, 'They shall die in the wilderness.' Not one of them survived, except Caleb the son of Jephunneh and Joshua the son of Nun" (Num 26:64–65).

The chapters that follow the second census (Numbers 27–36) differ sharply from what precedes, where murmuring and rebellion are prevalent. The focus here is on the fidelity of the new generation, which as a reward does not lose a single life, even in battle (31:49)!

The portrayal of Moses in Numbers is of particular interest. Betraying a streak of self-doubt (11:14), he indulges in self-pity (11:11,15) and even questions God (11:21–22). He becomes intemperate (20:10–11) and gives way to his anger to the point that he commits the ultimate heresy of attributing a miracle to himself (20:10). As we read about him, we feel we know this man Moses, for we recognize him in ourselves. He knows the meaning of burnout—he is worn out by the grueling tasks he faces day after day. Though the people are liberated from slavery in Egypt, they reveal that they are still slaves in their attitudes, and by their panic that the Promised Land promises only disaster (14:3). Moses cannot handle them. His leadership falters such that he cannot be entrusted to bring them into the Promised Land.

The literary relationship between Numbers and Genesis may be diagrammed in a nested menorah pattern, as follows:

Genesis and Numbers in a Menorah Pattern

A	The land promised to Abraham	Gen 12:7
B	Origins of Moab and Ammon by Lot seduced by his daughters	Gen 19:30–38
C	Two nations (Israel and Edom) struggling in Rebecca's womb	Gen 25:23
X	**Jacob/Israel poised to enter the Promised Land**	Gen 32–Num 20
C´	Balaam prophesies Edom's downfall [at the hands of David]	Num 24:18
B´	Israel seduced by the daughters of Moab	Num 25:1–6
A´	Land in Transjordan partitioned among Reuben, Gad and Manasseh	Num 32

2nd *Level Menorah: Israel Poised to Enter the Land*	*Genesis 32–Numbers 20*
A Esau (Edom) and Jacob (Israel) treat each other generously	Gen 32–33
B Jacob's last word (blessing) to his twelve sons	Gen 49
C Joseph confirms the promise of land	Gen 50:24
X Moses and the Exodus from Egypt—Tabernacle built	Exodus–Leviticus
C′ Census of Jacob's inheritors, the twelve tribes	Num 1
B′ Jacob's twelve sons placed around the Tabernacle	Num 2–3
A′ Edom refuses Israel's safe passage on route to the Promised Land	Num 20:14–21

Mary Douglas describes the relationship observed here as "Number's Commentary on Genesis."[1] It is easier to explain the nature of the dependence the other way around, with insertion of specific texts in Genesis to anticipate others in Numbers. At any rate, Exodus and Leviticus are framed by a series of parallel texts in Genesis and Numbers, which appear in a nested menorah pattern. These texts are concerned primarily with Israel's relationship with Edom, Moab and Ammon, from the time of Abraham (Gen 12:7) to the partition of Transjordan under Moses (Numbers 32).

Concept Check #16

How would you describe the difference in tone of Numbers before and after the second census in chapter 26?

Check your answer at the back of this book.

B. The Wilderness Encampment
Levites as Guards of the Tabernacle

One of the more interesting texts among the Dead Sea Scrolls presents an eschatological war of "the sons of light against the sons of darkness," which has as its backdrop the encampment of the hosts of Yahweh in the wilderness as described in Numbers 2.[2] In short, the concept of the battle camp in which the twelve tribes are arranged in four groups around the Tabernacle is still alive more than a thousand years after the time of Moses.

Some scholars argue that the arrangement of the people of Israel in battle formation around the Tabernacle in the biblical text reflects a festival in ancient Israel, perhaps Passover as it was celebrated in Gilgal near Jericho before the building of Solomon's Temple in Jerusalem. The focus of that festival was on what Frank Cross has called "the ritual Conquest,"[3] or what we call here the "Wars of Yahweh." The arrangement of the tribes symmetrically around the Tabernacle in ancient Israel may be diagrammed as follows:

---

1   Mary Douglas, *In the Wilderness: The Doctrine of Defilement in the Book of Numbers.* JSOT Supplement 158 (Sheffield Academic Press, 1993), pp.98-101.

2   See Y. Yadin, *The Scroll of the Wars of the Sons of Light Against the Sons of Darkness* (London: Oxford University Press, 1962), pp. 38-64.

3   F. M. Cross, Jr., *Canaanite Myth and Hebrew Epic* (Cambridge, MA: Harvard University Press, 1973), pp. 99-111.

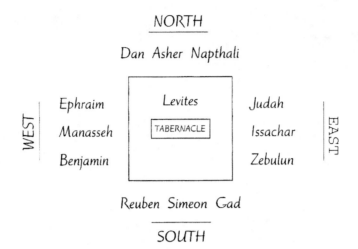

Encampment of the Tribes of Israel in "Holy War" around the Tabernacle
(Source: Mary Douglas [1993], p. 175)

The four groups of tribes are arranged according to the compass, with Judah as leader of the eastern contingent facing the entrance to the Tabernacle. Ephraim, the leader of the western group is located on the opposite side. Dan is the leader of the three tribes to the north and Reuben the leader of the three to the south. Moving clockwise from the entrance to the Tabernacle in the east, the first two groups are the five tribes of Leah (Judah, Issachar, Zebulun, Reuben and Simon) and Gad, the elder son of Leah's maid Zilpah. The three tribes to the west are the son (Benjamin) and grandsons of Rachel (i.e., the two sons of Joseph—Ephraim and Manasseh). Asher, the second of Zilpah's sons is in the group to the north, which also includes Dan and Naphtali, the two sons of Bilhah the maid of Rachel.

The camps of the Levites are arranged in order within the center of the battle camp, around the Tabernacle, as follows:

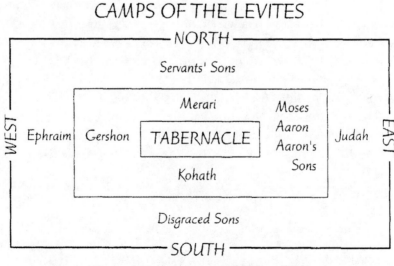

(Source: Mary Douglas [1993], p. 178)

Moses, Aaron, and Aaron's sons are located in the east directly in front of the entrance to the Tabernacle. Moving clockwise around the Tabernacle we find the descendants of the three sons of Levi: Kohath, Gershon, and Merari. Among these the Kohathites, as the most important group, are given responsibility for the Ark of the Covenant, the furniture (and vessels) of the Holy Place (i.e., the table of the bread of Presence, the menorah, the incense altar, and the veil to the Holy of Holies)

Though the biblical text focuses primarily on the Levites in terms of their responsibilities for transporting the tabernacle complex, including the Meeting Tent (with its coverings), they had other duties as well. The Hebrew phrase used to describe their duty *shammar mishmeret* (Num 31:30, 47), means to "keep guard." In short, they are the guards of the Tabernacle. In later tradition we find further evidence that supports this conclusion. In Herod's Temple, the Levitical watch was stationed at twenty-four specific points, according to the Mishnah (Tamid 1:1). According to Josephus, more than two hundred gatekeepers remained at their posts and were responsible for closing the gates of the Temple (Against Apion 2.119). Philo says that Levite guards made their rounds day and night to ensure the purity of the Temple (I Laws 156). In short, the term *mishmeret* as "guard duty" in Numbers refers to more than mere ceremonial duty. The Levites constitute the military guard responsible for the Tabernacle within the battle camp of ancient Israel.

Concept Check #17

How were the wars of Yahweh commemorated within the worship experience of the people of ancient Israel?

Check your answer at the back of this book.

C. Reading the Book of Numbers from the Center

Mary Douglas outlines Numbers in thirteen parts, which alternate between Story and Law in a series of "parallel rungs" in what she calls "the book in a ring."[4] The concentric structure she observes may be outlined in a nested menorah pattern:

The Book of Numbers in a Menorah Pattern	*Numbers 1–36*
A Story: Census of the 12 tribes, heirs to land and danger of encroachment	1:1–4:49
B Law: Keeping faith and breaking faith	5:1–6:27
C Story: Gifts to Yahweh and Yahweh's gifts to Aaron	7:1–8:26
X **Forty years in the wilderness—from Sinai to the plains of Moab**	9:1–30:16
C´ Story: Defeat of Midianite kings, booty purified; summary of journey	31:1–33:49
B´ Law: Destroy images, partition the Promised Land, cities of refuge	33:50–35:34
A´ Story: The sons of Joseph and the land [encroachment]	36:1–13

---

4   Ibid., p. 118.

2ⁿᵈ Level Menorah: From Sinai to the Plains of Moab   *Numbers 9–30*

A   Law: Passover; blowing trumpets and appointed feasts   9:1–10:10
B   Story: The Wilderness of Paran   10:11–14:45
C   Law: Offerings for priests, guilt and innocence   15:1–40
X   **Story: Encroachment punished, 12 rods subject to Aaron's rod** 16:1–17:13
C´   Law: Offerings for priests, cleansing from blood   18:1–19:22
B´   Story: The Wilderness of Zin   20:1–27:23
A´ Law: Appointed feasts [including Trumpets] and women's vows   28:1–30:16

The book of Numbers begins and ends with lengthy sections that present the people of Israel preparing to enter the Promised Land. In the first instance, they depart from Mount Sinai but fail to enter the land in spite of the guiding presence of Yahweh's cloud leading them day by day (Num 10:33–34). Their journey from Sinai to Kadesh-barnea is filled with complaining and even outright rebellion on the part of Aaron and Miriam who are jealous of their brother Moses (chaps. 11–12). When spies are sent into the land of Canaan, they bring back a discouraging report and the people refuse to enter the land (chap. 13). In spite of intercessory prayer in their behalf by Moses (chap. 14), the people of Israel are forced to spend forty years on the edge of the Promised Land. Eventually they launch out from Kadesh-barnea and make their way around Edom to the plains of Moab (chap. 21). There the first phase of the wars of Yahweh is completed with the conquest of the two Amorite kings, Sihon and Og. The tribes of Reuben, Gad, and half of Manasseh now possess their own land and the stage is set for another chapter in God's story. Preparations resume to enter the Promised Land; but this time the journey will take place under new leadership. A second census of the people marks the beginning of another lengthy section (chaps. 26–36), in which plans are made to enter the Promised Land by way of the Jordan Valley north of the Dead Sea.

1. The Ten Parashoth in the Book of Numbers

Though there is a great deal of merit in the arguments of Mary Douglas to see Numbers in the structural form of a "book in a ring," her model is somewhat forced in the alternating sections of law throughout the book. A more useful portrayal of the structure of the book of Numbers as a whole emerges from reflection on the boundaries of the Parashoth (weekly portions in the annual cycle of readings from the Torah). The scribes of antiquity apparently divided the book into three major parts, each of which may be outlined in a menorah pattern:

➤ Preparing to enter the Promised Land   Num 1:1–12:16   Parashoth 34–36

➤ From "unholy war" to the Wars of Yahweh   Num 13:1–25:9   Parashoth 37–40

➤ Preparing for life in the Promised Land   Num 25:10–36:13 Parashoth 41–43

Parashoth 34–36: Preparing to Enter the Promised Land — Num 1:1–12:16

A	Military census and arrangement of the wilderness camp	1:1–2:34
B	Census of the Levites	3:1–4:49
C	Purification of the camp	5:1–6:27
X	**Offerings from tribal leaders and consecration of the Levites**	**7:1–8:26**
C´	Second observance of Passover (at Sinai)—the journey begins	9:1–23
B´	Instructions on blowing trumpets to signal Israel is on the march	10:1–10
A´	The trek from Sinai to Kadesh	10:11–12:16

Parashoth 37–40: From "Unholy War" to the Wars of Yahweh — Num 13:1–25:9

A	The reconnaissance of Canaan and Israel's unholy war	13:1–14:45
B	Cultic regulations	15:1–41
C	Encroachment on the part of Korah, Dathan, Abiram and On	16:1–50
X	**Aaron's budding rod—shows special status of his priesthood**	**17:1–12**
C´	Responsibility of Aaronic priesthood and other Levites	18:1–32
B´	Purification from contamination by a corpse	19:1–22
A´	The trek from Kadesh to Shittim and the wars of Yahweh	20:1–25:18

Parashoth 41–43: Preparing for Life in the Promised Land — Num 25:10–36:13

A	From sin at Peor to Zelophehad's daughters (inheritance rights)	25:10–27:11
B	Joshua commissioned to succeed Moses for Eisodus into Cisjordan	27:12–23
C	Cultic calendar for life in the land [+ addendum on vows]	28:1–30:16
X	**Holy war vs. Midian—cleansing the contamination of Peor**	**31:1–54**
C´	Allotment of land in Transjordan	32:1–42
B´	The trek from Egypt to the Jordan for Eisodus into Cisjordan	33:1–35:34
A´	Heiresses must marry within their clan (Zelophehad's daughters)	36:1–13

In this reading, the focus in the first two sections (Parashoth 34–40) is on the consecration of the Levites and the special status of Aaron's priesthood within the tribe of Levi. The focus on the holy war against Midian in the third section (Parashoth 41–43) sets the stage for the presentation of the "wars of Yahweh," which follows—i.e., the Eisodus into the Promised Land under Moses and Joshua.

It is instructive to outline Numbers in a nested menorah pattern that focuses attention on the narrative (story) sections, and the journey from Sinai to the plains of Moab in particular:

The Book of Numbers in a Menorah Pattern — Numbers 1–36

A	The people of God prepare to enter the Promised Land	1:1–10:10
B	Journey from Sinai to Kadesh-barnea	10:11–12:16
C	The reconnaissance of Canaan and Israel's unholy war	13:1–14:45
X	**Encroachment on the Tabernacle—special status of Aaron**	**15:1–19:22**
C´	Planned detour through Edom	20:1–21
B´	Journey from Kadesh-barnea to the plains of Moab	20:22–25:18
A´	The people of God prepare to enter the Promised Land	26:1–36:16

2nd *Level Menorah: Encroachment on the Tabernacle*	*Num 15:1–19:22*
A Cultic regulation	15:1–41
B Revolts against Moses—Korah, Dathan, Abiram and On	16:1–40
C People rebel against Moses and Aaron; God sends a plague	16:41–50
X **Aaron's budding rod—shows special status of his priesthood**	17:1–11
C´ People complain: "We are perishing, we are lost"	17:12–13
B´ Responsibility of Aaronic priesthood and other Levites	18:1–32
A´ Rites for purifying a person who is defiled by a corpse	19:1–22

In this reading, the two major sections on laws become a framework around the second-level menorah pattern (chaps. 15–19), which is spelled out in greater detail. The content of the other sections in the primary menorah structure may also be explored in menorah patterns.

2. Preparing to Enter the Promised Land (Num 1:1–10:10)

The opening section of the book of Numbers, which concerns the organization of the wilderness camp for the journey to the Promised Land, may be outlined in a nested menorah pattern, as follows:

The People of God Prepare to Enter the Promised Land	*Num 1:1–10:10*
A Military census in the wilderness of Sinai (excluding Levi)	1:1–54
B The arrangement of the camp (excluding Levites)	2:1–34
C Census of the Levites	3:1–4:49
X **Purification of the camp**	5:1–6:27
C´ Offerings from tribal leaders and consecration of Levites	7:1–8:26
B´ Second observance of Passover (at Sinai)—the journey begins	9:1–23
A´ Instructions for blowing trumpets to signal Israel is on the march	10:1–10

The outermost frame here opens with a military census of the tribes of Israel, except for Levi (1:1–54). It concludes with a brief section on the blowing of special trumpets by "the sons of Aaron, the priests," to signal that the people of Israel are on the march (10:1–10). The second frame opens with an account of the arrangement of the tribes symmetrically around the Meeting Tent (Tabernacle). It concludes with an observance of Passover, after which the journey from Mount Sinai to the Promised Land begins (9:1–23). The innermost frame focuses on the Levites, who are first numbered in a census of their own (3:1–4:49), and then consecrated after tribal leaders present their offerings and dedicate the altar (7:1–8:26). In the center we find a section on the purification of the camp (5:1–6:27), which is explored in detail in a second-level menorah pattern, as follows:

2nd *Level Menorah: Purification of the Camp*	*Numbers 5–6*
A Sanctity of the Tabernacle—excluding those who are impure	5:1–4
B Case law: breaking faith when there is no next of kin	5:5–10
C Case of a woman suspected of adultery—the facts of the case	5:11–14
X **The ritual ordeal to determine guilt or innocence**	5:15–28
C´ Case of a woman suspected of adultery—presumptive subscript	5:29–31
B´ Case law: the Nazirite vow—for innocent contamination by a corpse	6:1–21
A´ Aaronic benediction: "May Yahweh bless you and keep you"	6:22–27

This nested menorah pattern converges on the curious case of a ritual ordeal to determine the guilt or innocence of a woman suspected of adultery (5:15–28). If the principle of the "riddle in the middle" applies, one wonders if there is symbolic meaning here. Is Israel herself to be taken as the woman in question, in her covenant relationship with Yahweh?

3. Journey from Mount Sinai to Transjordan (Num 10:11–22:1)

The account of Israel's journey from Sinai to Transjordan may be outlined in a nested menorah pattern, as follows:

The Journey from Sinai to Transjordan	*Num 10:11–22:1*
A From Sinai to Kadesh	10:11–12:16
B The reconnaissance of Canaan and Israel's unholy war	13:1–14:45
C Cultic regulations	15:1–41
X **Encroachment on the Tabernacle—special status of Aaron**	16:1–18:32
C´ Purification from contamination by a corpse	19:1–22
B´ Planned detour through Edom—to get to the Promised Land	20:1–21
A´ From Kadesh to the plains of Moab	20:22–22:1

The outermost frame in this reading moves from Sinai to Kadesh, on the one hand (10:11–12:16), and from Kadesh to the plains of Moab, on the other (20:22–22:1). The second frame opens with the account of the sending of twelve spies to spy out the land of Canaan, their bad report, and Israel's subsequent abortive attempt to enter the land of Canaan (13:1–14:45). It continues with their unsuccessful request to pass through the land of Edom on route to the Promised Land (20:1–21). The innermost frame consists of two parallel chapters on matters of cultic regulation (15:1–41 and 19:1–22). The middle section in this menorah pattern, which is also the structural center of the book of Numbers as a whole, takes up the matter of encroachment on the part of priestly rivals and the special status of Aaron within the Levitical priesthood (16:1–18:32). This section is explored in detail as a "wheel within a wheel"—another menorah pattern:

2nd *Level Menorah: Encroachment on the Tabernacle*	*Numbers 16–18*
A Revolts against Moses—Korah, Dathan, Abiram and On	16:1–40
B People rebel against Moses and Aaron	16:41–45
C Aaron takes incense in a censer and stays the plague	16:46–50
X **Test of the rods—one from each of the twelve tribes**	17:1–7
C´ Aaron's rod budded and produced ripe almonds	17:8–11
B´ People complain: "We are perishing, we are lost"	17:12–13
A´ Laws on provisioning the cult	18:1–32

The miracle of the budding of Aaron's rod sets him apart as God's chosen leader in the priestly establishment (17:1–7). It is interesting to note how similar the structural center of Numbers is to that of Deuteronomy (Deut 18:1–8). Both passages are concerned with provisioning the cultic establishment and the priority of Levitical priests descended from Aaron.

> ### Concept Check #18
>
> What is the significance of Mount Hor in the wilderness journeys of ancient Israel?
>
> Check your answer at the back of this book.

4. Preparing for Life in the Promised Land (Numbers 26–36)

The third major section in Numbers may also be outlined in a nested menorah pattern:

The People of God Prepare to Enter the Promised Land	*Numbers 26–36*
A Second military census—of the new generation of warriors	26:1–65
B The law of succession in inheritance	27:1–11
C The succession of Moses by Joshua	27:12–23
X Calendar of public sacrifices + an addendum on vows	28:1–30:1
C´ The war against Midian	31:1–54
B´ The settlement of Transjordan	32:1–42
A´ Trek from Egypt to the Jordan River for the Eisodus into Canaan	33:1–36:13

A second military census is taken in the plains of Moab (26:1–65), which is set over against a summation of the trek from Egypt to the Jordan River in forty-two stages (33:1–56). That journey, which began at Ramses (in Egypt, on the day after the original Passover celebration), took them to Mount Nebo, where Moses died (33:1–56). The text continues with a presentation of the ideal boundaries of the Promised Land (34:1–29), and division of that land, including plans for Levitical cities and cities of asylum (35:1–34). The law of succession in inheritance (27:1–11) is set over against the actual inheritance of the land in Transjordan by the tribes of Reuben, Gad, and half of the tribe of Manasseh (32:1–42). The innermost frame moves from the succession of Joshua as Moses' successor (27:12–23), to an account of the war against Midian in which Eleazar, the son and successor of Aaron, plays a dominant role in the distribution of booty (31:1–54).

In the middle of the above menorah pattern, we find a detailed presentation of the calendar of public sacrifices for life in the Promised Land, which may be outlined in another menorah pattern:

2ⁿᵈ Level Menorah: The Cultic Calendar for Life in the Land	*Numbers 28–30*
A Public offerings—daily, Sabbath and the new moon	28:1–15
B Paschal sacrifice and Unleavened Bread and the Feast of Weeks	28:16–31
C *Rosh Hashanah*—first day of the seventh month	29:1–6
X Day of Atonement—tenth day of the seventh month	29:7–11
C´ Festival of *Sukkot*—15ᵗʰ to the 21ˢᵗ of the seventh month	29:12–34
B´ Sacrifices on the eighth day of *Sukkot* (Booths)	29:35–38
A´ Private offerings may be presented as well + addendum on vows	29:39–30:17

The concentric structure of Num 28:1–29:40 converges on the high holy days of the fall festival, and on the tenth day of Tishri in particular—the Day of Atonement (29:7–11).

> ## Concept Check #19
>
> What is the significance of Mount Nebo and what is its relation-
> ship to the second phase of the wars of Yahweh?
>
> Check your answer at the back of this book.

D. Numbers and the "Book of the Wars of Yahweh" (Num 21:14)

The Book of the Wars of Yahweh is mentioned only once in the Bible—in Num 21:14, where it is cited to settle a boundary dispute shortly before the conquest of the Amorite kingdom of Sihon. The document in question was not a "book" as such, at least in the way we think about books today. It was a scroll, or perhaps merely a familiar oral tradition—for no copy of this document has ever been found.

The narrator cites *The Book of the Wars of Yahweh* primarily because it places the boundary of Moab at the Arnon River. Though the Hebrew text is difficult to interpret, it may be rendered as follows:

> The Benefactor (i.e., Yahweh) has come in a storm;
> Indeed, he has come to the wadis of the Arnon.
> He marched through the wadis;
> He marched, he turned aside—to the seat of Ar;
> He leaned toward the border of Moab.

Because of archaic features, the Hebrew text was subsequently misread with resultant confusion in the ancient versions and modern translations.

The picture presented in this poem is that of the Divine Warrior (Yahweh) poised on the edge of the Promised Land, before the most celebrated battles of the Eisodus into the Promised Land. He has come in the whirlwind with his hosts to the sources of the Arnon River in Transjordan. He marches through the wadi valleys, turning aside to settle affairs with Moab before marching on against the two Amorite kings to the north, and then across the Jordan River to the battle camp at Gilgal and the conquest of the land of Canaan in Cisjordan. The picture is indeed a fitting one for the *incipit* (opening phrase in an old text) of a narrative poem entitled *The Book of the Wars of Yahweh*.

The wars of Yahweh were commemorated in ancient Israel in public worship, in some ways somewhat parallel to what Christian communities have done with the Eucharist, which is a symbolic portrayal of the death of the Messiah Yeshua (Jesus Christ). The people of ancient Israel remembered the wars of Yahweh as the primary salvational event in their history. These wars have two phases: the Exodus from Egypt and the Eisodus (Entry) into the Promised Land. The Eisodus takes place in two parts—under Moses in Transjordan and Joshua in Cisjordan.

The primary battles of the Exodus from Egypt focus on the defeat of Pharaoh at the crossing of the Sea (Exodus 14–15) and the defeat of the Amalekites on the way to Mount

Sinai (Exod 17:8–15). They also include the defeat of the king of Arad (Num 21:1–3) and the Midianites (Numbers 31). The defeat of the two Amorite kings, Sihon and Og, whose land was occupied by the Transjordanian tribes of Reuben, Gad, and Manasseh (east) belongs to this first phase of the Eisodus (Entry) into the Promised Land.

It should be noted that Joshua is presented as the military commander in Israel under Moses' leadership as early as the battle against the Amalekites in Exod 17:8–13. Thus it is also possible to consider all of the battles from the crossing of *Yam Suf* (Sea of Reeds) to the crossing of the Jordan River as the first phase of the Eisodus into the Promised Land. The second phase of the Eisodus takes place after the death of Moses, as Joshua becomes the instrument of Yahweh in the conquest of the land of the Canaanites (Cisjordan) recorded in Joshua 1–12.

To some extent, the Eisodus continues in Judges and 1 Samuel. David completes the conquest of the whole of the Promised Land, when he establishes the Davidic Empire. Though it is useful to think of David's achievement as an extension of the wars of Yahweh, *The Book of the Wars of Yahweh* appears to have focused specifically on the mighty acts of God in the days of Moses and Joshua.

Concept Check #20

Can you think of a reason that might explain why the "Book of the Wars of Yahweh," which is cited in Num 21:14, has never been found?

Check your answer at the back of this book.

E. Numbers within the Primary History
Evidence for a "Master Editor"

David Noel Freedman presents a strong case to support his belief that a master editor compiled the Primary History (the Torah and the Former Prophets).[5] Evidence for this conclusion is found in a series of episodes distributed book by book through eight successive books in the Tanakh that chart the violation of the first nine Commandments one by one. The series starts with the sin of national apostasy (the Golden Calf episode, Exodus 32), which violates the First and the Second Commandments, and concludes with the sin of bearing false witness (the Ninth Commandment) in the story of Naboth in 1 Kings 21. Because covetousness lies behind all the crimes committed, each act implicitly breaks the Tenth Commandment as well. The Ten Commandments constitute the essence of the covenant relationship established between God and the people of Israel at Mount Sinai. The pattern of defiance of that covenant with God led inexorably to the downfall of the nation of Israel, the destruction of the Temple, and the banishment of survivors from the Promised Land.

---

5   D. N. Freedman, *The Nine Commandments: Uncovering the Hidden Pattern of Crime and Punishment in the Hebrew Bible* (Doubleday, 2000).

Genesis does not include an episode in this series because the covenant at Mount Sinai, in which the stone tablets with the Ten Commandments are given to Moses, takes place later—in Exodus. The Commandments and their violations within the Primary history are as follows:

Commandment	Text	Episode
1. Do not worship other gods	Exodus 32	Golden Calf incident
2. No idols	Exodus 32	Golden Calf incident
3. Taking Yahweh's name in vain	Lev 24:10–17	Stoning to death for sin of blasphemy
4. Keep the Sabbath	Num 15:32–36	Stoning to death for violating the Sabbath
5. Honor your parents	Deut 21:18–21	Stoning to death of stubborn and rebellious son
6. You shall not steal	Josh 7:20–26	Stoning of Achan and his family for theft
7. You shall not murder	Judg 20:34–48	Murder of the Levite's concubine
8. You shall not commit adultery	2 Samuel 11	David and Bathsheba
9. You shall not bear false witness	1 Kings 21	Ahab, Jezebel, and Naboth's vineyard

The message in this sequence of texts is clear to a community in the Babylonian Exile. Their fate is not the result of God's abandoning them, but a consequence of their abandonment of God. By violating each one of the Ten Commandments, one after the other, the people of Israel have broken their covenant with Yahweh. The true people of God are those who maintain the covenant commitment to God by observing the Ten Commandments.

Concept Check #21

What are the implications of the evidence for a "master editor" of the Primary History on the question of the authorship of the Torah?

Check your answer at the back of this book.

The Pentateuchal Structure of the Book of Numbers

[Four Wheels of the Same Likeness and a Wheel within the Four Wheels]

A   The People of God Prepare to Enter the Promised Land   *Numbers 1–10*

a	Preparations for the departure from Sinai [1st census]	1:1–6:27
b	Offerings for the Tabernacle altar from tribal chieftains	7:1–89
x	Dedication of the Levites	8:1–26
b´	The second Passover—observed at Mount Sinai	9:1–23
a´	The departure from Sinai	10:1–36

B   The Journey from Mount Sinai to Kadesh   *Numbers 11–12*

a	People complain about manna and Moses shares leadership with 70 elders	11:1–17
b	Promise of meat to satisfy "craving"	11:18–23
x	Prophesying on the part of 70 elders (with Eldad and Medad)	11:24–30
b´	Promise fulfilled with quails to satisfy "craving"	11:31–35
a´	Political rebellion on the part of Miriam and Aaron	12:1–16

X   Forty Years on the Edge of the Promised Land   *Numbers 13–20*

a	Disaster at Kadesh (rebellion of the spies and Israel's "unholy war")	13:1–14:45
b	Laws on offerings	15:1–41
x	Special status of the Levitical priests	16:1–18:32
b´	Laws on cleansing	19:1–22
a´	Death of Miriam, "rebellion" of Moses at Meribah, and death of Aaron	20:1–29

B´   The Journey from Kadesh to the Plains of Moab   *Numbers 21–25*

a	Defeat of Arad in battle of Hormah (wars of Yahweh)	21:1–3
b	Journey around Edom to the Arnon Valley (the bronze serpent)	21:4–20
x	Holy war against Amorite kings—defeat of Sihon and Og	21:21–35
b´	In the plains of Moab—Balak summons Balaam to curse Israel	22:1–24:25
a´	National apostasy at Shittim in Moab (worship of Baal of Peor)	25:1–18

A´   The People of God Prepare to Enter the Promised Land   *Numbers 26–36*

a	Preparation for the departure from Shittim [2nd census]	26:1–65
b	Property laws, offerings, and vows (daughters of Zelophehad)	27:1–30:16
x	Waging holy war against Midian (wars of Yahweh)	31:1–54
b´	Property in Transjordan allotted to Reuben, Gad and Manasseh	32:1–42
a´	Preparation for the Eisodus: stages of journey from Egypt and directions	33:1–36:13

Study Questions

These study questions are optional and are designed for the student who wishes to go beyond what is required. *Do not send them to the Center for evaluation.*

1. What were the various complaints of the Israelites in Numbers 11–14? What gave rise to them and what were the results? What does this teach about murmuring in our lives today?

2. What light does Hebrews 3 shed on the failure to enter the land in Numbers 13 and 14?

3. Compare Num 21:4–9 with John 3:14–15. How many parallels can you find between the incident with the serpents and the work of Yeshua (Jesus)?

4. Why did God perform such extreme miracles in the day so Numbers? Are such miracles observed today? Why or why not?

5. What was the sin of Moses at Meribah (Num 20:9–13)?

6. Hebrews 3–4 applies Numbers to the life of God's people in another setting. Even as the people of Israel needed to watch their lives and keep right with God on their journey to Canaan, if they would enter the land, so we must "be diligent to enter that rest" (Heb 4:11). What is the spiritual "rest" God offers to those who fulfill his conditions?

5

The Book of Deuteronomy

Contents

A. Deuteronomy as the Center of the Canonical Process
B. The Musical Composition of Deuteronomy
C. Reading the Book of Deuteronomy from the Center
D. The Numerical Composition of Deuteronomy
E. Law and Narrative in the Bible

Objectives

When this chapter is completed, the student should be able to:

♦ Explain how Deuteronomy functions as the center of the canonical process

♦ Identify and explain the "Principle Commandment" in the book of Deuteronomy

♦ Explain the relationship between the Ten Commandments and the laws in Deuteronomy 12–25

♦ Explain the significance of Mount Gerizim and Mount Ebal in ancient Israel

♦ Discuss the evidence for and significance of the numerical composition of Deuteronomy

A. Deuteronomy as the Center of the Canonical Process

The name of the fifth book of the Torah in Jewish tradition is דברים (pronounced *Devarim* ("words"), shortened from *'elleh haddevarim*, "these are the words"—the first two words of the Hebrew text. The name Deuteronomy comes from the Septuagint translation of Deut 17:18, which refers to a "repetition (*deuteronomium* in Greek) of this Torah." The Hebrew text actually instructs the king to make "a copy of this Torah." Within its present canonical context, Deuteronomy is indeed a repetition of the Torah of Moses as delivered earlier at Mount Sinai (Horeb) in the books of Exodus through Numbers. It is also a literary bridge connecting the first two major divisions of the Tanakh—the Torah and the Prophets. This is particularly true in regards the close connection between Deuteronomy and the book of Joshua, which is the first of the four books in the Former Prophets: Joshua, Judges, Samuel (in two parts), and Kings (in two parts).

In Jewish tradition, God made the original copy of the Ten Commandments on two tablets of stone in the twilight of the sixth day of Creation, as an afterthought—along with a number of other items he would need later for special moments in the unfolding story. Such items include the ram he would use to take the place of Isaac in the *Akedah* (Genesis 22), and the Great Fish in the story of Jonah. In poetic language, this is a way of saying that God's revelation in written form, which culminates in the completion of the Tanakh (Torah, Prophets and Writings), starts with the Ten Commandments at the very beginning.

The central historical event in the shaping of the epic story in the Tanakh is the deliverance of the people of Israel from slavery in Egypt (the Exodus). Regardless of how one chooses to reconstruct the historical details of this event, the Exodus from Egypt constitutes the starting point in explaining the canonical process in ancient Israel. The event of the Exodus from Egypt calls for its counterpart in the Eisodus (Entry) into the Promised Land. The people who came out of Egypt under Moses begin an epic journey, which eventually brings them "home" to the Promised Land, under the leadership of Joshua. In the previous chapter, we suggested that the "Book of the Wars of Yahweh" in Num 21:14 is a descriptive title of that epic story. The "wars of Yahweh" are divided into two phases: the Exodus under Moses and the Eisodus under Joshua.

The Exodus involves a journey from *Yam Suf* ("Sea of Reeds") to the Jordan River in three stages. The great theophany at Sinai, in which the presence of the Divine Warrior is revealed to Israel through Moses, is framed by two accounts of wilderness journeys. On the one hand, we have the trek from Egypt to Mount Sinai and, on the other, from Mount Sinai to Mount Nebo and the transfer of leadership from Moses to Joshua. Edward Newing has shown that the "Promised Presence," as depicted in Exod 33:1–17, is in the center of the first major section of the canon in the Tanakh. As Newing puts it, the journey from Egypt to Canaan is in three stages: 1) "From Slavery/Promise," to 2) the great theophany ("Promised Presence") on the Mountain of God at Sinai/Horeb, and from there 3) "To Freedom/Fulfillment."[1]

Wholeness in depth psychology is normally expressed in quaternary, or four-part, structures. The four elements in any given structure tend to be arranged in a chiasm. At the same time, three of the four are generally set over against the fourth. The final arrangement of the canon of the Tanakh still reflects an earlier "three plus one" structuring of the tradition within the developing canonical process.

Exodus	Leviticus	Joshua	Judges
Numbers	Deuteronomy	Samuel	Kings

Here the three "wilderness books" (Exodus, Leviticus, and Numbers) are supplemented by a "second recitation of the law" (Deuteronomy) on the part of Moses, immediately prior to his death. Joshua in turn stands over against the story of the possession of the Promised Land under a series of twelve judges, followed by the united monarchy under David and Solomon (with the building of the Temple in Jerusalem), and the subsequent divided monarchy. The chiastic relationship within this pair of pairs should be noted. As R. D. Nelson has shown, Joshua and Josiah are paired as an envelope, or inclusion, around what eventually comes to be known as the Former Prophets within the canonical process.[2]

1   E. Newing, "A Rhetorical and Theological Analysis of the Hexateuch," *South East Asia Journal of Theology* 22 (1981), pp. 1-15.

2   R. D. Nelson, "Josiah in the Book of Joshua," *Journal of Biblical Literature* 100 (1977), pp. 531-540.

The "Moses Story" (Exodus through Deuteronomy) and the Former Prophets are subsequently framed by two blocks of material, which become the book of Genesis and the Latter Prophets. Once again, it is easy to see the "three plus one" structuring within these categories in terms of the final canonical shaping of the tradition:

"Patriarchs"   =   Abraham, Isaac, Jacob   +   Jacob's twelve sons

"Prophets"   =   Isaiah, Jeremiah, Ezekiel   +   "Book of the Twelve"

At this point, the center in the developing canonical process shifts to the book of Deuteronomy, which functions as a bridge connecting four groups of four books, in what we call the seventeen-book (or Deuteronomic) canon of the Bible, as follows:

Genesis	Exodus		Joshua	Judges
Leviticus	Numbers		Samuel	Kings
		Deuteronomy		
Isaiah	Jeremiah		Psalms	Job
Ezekiel	"The Twelve"		Proverbs	*Megilloth*

The *Megilloth* are the Festal Scrolls, which ultimately become five in number: Ruth, Song of Solomon, Lamentations, Ecclesiastes, and Esther.

The four sections of the above structure represent the four primary canonical divisions, which are arranged in a chiasm, with Deuteronomy functioning as a bridge between them.

Torah	Former Prophets
Latter Prophets	Hagiographa

It should be noted, however, that when the deuteronomic canon first emerges in the sixth century BCE, the fourth category does not yet include Esther, Daniel, Ezra, Nehemiah, and 1–2 Chronicles, which appear later in time. The seven books in the Hagiographa are Psalms, Job, Proverbs, Ruth, Song of Solomon, Lamentations, and Ecclesiastes. At this point, the canon is "open" in the sense that additions can be made within the fourth category, which eventually becomes the "Writings" of the Tanakh.

Concept Check #22

What is the relationship of Deuteronomy to the other books in the Torah and the Former Prophets?

Check your answer at the back of this book.

B. The Musical Composition of Deuteronomy

As Bishop Robert Lowth noted more than two centuries ago, the law codes throughout the Mediterranean world were sung at the festivals in antiquity.[3]

> It is evident that Greece for several successive ages was possessed of no records but the poetic: for the first who published a prose oration was Pherecydes, a man of the Isle of Syrus, and the contemporary with king Cyrus, who lived some ages posterior to that of Homer and Hesiod: somewhat after the time of Cadmus the Milesian began to compose history. The laws themselves were metrical, and adapted to certain musical notes: such were the laws of Charondas, which were sung at the banquets of the Athenians: such were those which were delivered by the Cretans to the ingenuous youth to be learned by rote, with the accompaniments of musical melody, in order that by the enchantment of harmony, the sentiments might be forcibly impressed upon their memories. Hence certain poems were denominated *nomoi* which implied convivial or banqueting songs, as is remarked by Aristotle; who adds, that the same custom of chanting the laws to music, existed even in his own time among the Agathyrsi.

The law book we call Deuteronomy was in the hands of the Levites (Deut 17:18) who were commanded by Moses to recite it at the Festival of Booths (Deut 31:9). Though we do not know the precise nature of this performance of the text, it is likely that it was sung and that this greater "Song of Moses" (i.e., the entire book of Deuteronomy) was taught to the people. For generations Deuteronomy was recited in Levitical circles as a primary means of religious education. Eventually it was put in written form and promulgated in Jerusalem as part of a reform movement in the days of King Josiah. Within that movement, Deuteronomy became the center of a canonical process that eventually produced the Tanakh as we now have it. That canonical text was recited within the musical tradition of the Second Temple in Jerusalem. The memory of that tradition is still reflected in the Masoretic accentual system of the Hebrew Bible and the practice of canting the weekly portions of the readings from the Torah in Jewish synagogues to the present day.

For centuries now the main stream of the scholarly community has virtually ignored the Masoretic accentual system so far as detailed analysis and commentary on the text of the Hebrew Bible are concerned. There is widespread agreement that the system is essentially a form of musical notation of some sort. At the same time, most scholars argue that the system is medieval in origin and imposed on the Hebrew text—perhaps as a form of chant to recite the text in a liturgical setting. After all, the so-called tropes of this Masoretic system are still used to instruct those who cant the text within the various synagogue traditions.

For some years now, the musicologist Suzanne Haïk-Vantoura has championed the idea that these cantillation signs represent an ancient tradition of musical interpretation, which predates the Masoretes by a millenium, or more.[4] Haïk-Vantoura argues convinc-

---

3   R. Lowth, *Lectures on the Sacred Poetry of the Hebrews*, trans. G. Gregory (London: Chadwick, 1815), pp. 54-55.

4   S. Haïk-Vantoura, *The Music of the Bible Revealed*, tr. D. Weber and ed. J. Wheeler (Berkeley: BIBAL Press, 1991).

ingly that the Masoretes did not invent the musical tradition reflected in their sophisticated system of notation. They merely fixed on paper a once living tradition so as to preserve it for all time. The source of their knowledge was apparently the "Elders of Bathyra," certain sages among the predecessors of the Karaite community during the first century CE.[5] Haïk-Vantoura attempts to recover the actual melodies of what she believes were part of the text of the Hebrew Bible in the period of the Second Temple in ancient Israel, and earlier, which the Masoretes themselves only partially understood. Though they were aware of the fact that the system represents a rich musical heritage, they themselves were not musicians. Consequently, they focused their attention primarily on the linguistic features of that system and used it to work out elaborate grammatical treatises on the accentual system they had inherited.

It should be noted that music and poetry are a common medium for transmitting cultural tradition among virtually all preliterate peoples. In light of this fact, some missionaries and administrators of mission agencies are asking new questions about the translation of the Bible into previously unwritten languages. The model of the Wycliffe Bible translator has been challenged in recent years from within the ranks of those translators, as the most effective means of communicating the word of God in such situations. Should an individual give virtually a lifetime to the tedious task of reducing such a language to written form in order to translate the Bible into one more of the two thousand such languages that exist to the present time? Where this has been done, the Bible sometimes remains an external artifact that never really becomes a vital part of the cultural tradition of these tribal groups. Would it not be better to translate the Bible into media already present in such societies for the transmission of culture, namely into their own forms of music? Experiments with the oral communication of the Scripture in sub-Saharan Africa, as reported by Herbert Klem,[6] suggest a positive answer to this question. Moreover, it may well be that these very experiments provide a closer analogue to the historical situation in ancient Israel than the several models advanced within the mainstream of academic study of the Bible.

In short, Deuteronomy is best explained as a didactic poem, composed to be recited publicly to music in ancient Israel within a liturgical setting. The book is primarily a work of literary art designed to transmit a canonical body of tradition as effectively as possible to a given people. It was composed for oral recitation and, as models in the field of ethnomusicology suggest, was composed with music as an essential aspect of the tradition itself. Moreover, as a work of literary art, Deuteronomy was consciously composed in what some call an "epic style," which is similar in its structural features to other epic texts in the world of antiquity. Thus we ought not to be surprised to find concentric structural features, which are also the subject of investigation by students of Homer's *Iliad* and Virgil's *Aeneid*. And indeed such features are present in the biblical text, as witnessed by the spate of such observations emerging in the field of biblical studies in recent years.

---

5   See P. Kahle, *The Cairo Geniza*, 2nd ed. (New York: Praeger, 1959), 82-86, 103.

6   H. Klem, *Oral Communication of the Scriptures: Insights from African Oral Art* (Pasadena: William Carey Library, 1982).

Recent research in Deuteronomy suggests that the Hebrew text in its present form, as preserved by the Masoretes, is a musical composition. The canting tradition of the synagogues preserves memory of the original performance of the text during the period of the Second Temple in Jerusalem, and perhaps earlier, as Haïk-Vantoura insists.

An important aspect of the earlier stages of that canonical process is suggested by the work of Milman Perry and Albert Lord in their oral-formulaic theory, which is based on field work among Yugoslavian poet/musicians.[7] The idea of "oral composition-in-performance," for instance, is a useful model to explain the transmission of the *Iliad* from the time of Homer to the fixing of that text in written form centuries later in ancient Greece. Frank Cross and some of his students posit a somewhat parallel phenomenon in their arguments for the presumed "Hebrew Epic" that lies behind the Pentateuch as we now have it.[8] Richard Martin's work opens perhaps another chapter in this fascinating story.[9] Martin builds his investigation primarily on the basis of the disciplines of text linguistics and classical rhetoric, which include careful attention to the new performance-centered approach to verbal art that takes into account the audience for which the speech-act was composed.[10] Martin notes at the outset of his study that, in the final analysis, it does not matter whether Homer's *Iliad* is a piece of oral poetry or not. We simply do not have an oral *Iliad*, "because the poem has somehow become a text; and that has made all the difference. To put it another way, our *Iliad* is no longer an action, as it must have been if it was ever an oral composition-in-performance. Instead, it is an artifact." The same is true of the book of Deuteronomy.

Deuteronomy is the center of a complex process of canonical activity, from at least the time of King Josiah to the dedication of the Second Temple in Jerusalem at the end of the sixth century BCE. In my opinion, Deuteronomy enjoys generations of use within public worship in ancient Israel, in the hands of Levitical singers in ancient Israel, *before* its use at the center of canonical activity in the time of Josiah. That canonical process includes much more than the mere compilation of the Torah. It also includes the Former Prophets within a larger canonical entity that D. N. Freedman calls the "Primary History."[11] It may have included both the Latter Prophets and the Writings as canonical categories as well, though perhaps not in the form we now know.

T. Georgiades, a music historian, has shown convincingly, at least for ancient Greek literature, that the distinct concepts of music and poetry as we understand them today were not known in antiquity: "The ancient Greek verse line was a singular formation for which there is no analogy in Western Christian civilization. It was, if you will, music and poetry in one, and precisely because of this it could not be separated into music and poetry as two tangibly distinct components. For this particular vehicle of meaning the Greeks, however, had a special term μουσική" [from which the English word "music" is

---

7   See A. B. Lord, *The Singer of Tales* (Cambridge: Harvard University Press, 1960).

8   F. M. Cross, *Canaanite Myth and Hebrew Epic* (Cambridge: Harvard University Press, 1973).

9   R. P. Martin, *The Language of Heroes: Speech and Performance in the Iliad* (Ithaca: Cornell University Press, 1989).

10 See E. Fine, *The Folklore Text: From Performance to Print* (Bloomington: Indiana University Press, 1984).

11 D. N. Freedman, "Canon of the OT," in *The Interpreter's Dictionary of the Bible: Supplementary Volume* (Nashville: Abingdon Press, 1976), 131-132.

derived].[12] The work of S. Haïk-Vantoura is essentially built on the same observation. As with ancient Greek literature, the Hebrew Bible emerged in the form of μουσική—a combination of music and language. What is unique about the situation in ancient Israel is the fact that the canonical form of the musical performance of the biblical text is apparently recoverable, at least in part. Aspects of that speech-act, which is in the form of a musical performance of considerable sophistication, opens the door to a new set of questions we may now address to the study of the biblical text.

In a fundamental sense, then, Deuteronomy in its entirety may be described as "poetry" in the broadest sense. Though it contains a lyric "Song of Moses" (Deut 32), most of the book is in the form of didactic poetry of a lesser nature so far as heightened speech goes. The composer of the original was Moses, but the text itself enjoyed a life of its own for generations within the public worship of ancient Israel. Individual words no doubt changed in usage through time. Indeed, the very structure of the greater "Song of Moses," which we now call the book of Deuteronomy, may have changed as it developed in public performance by a long line of singers in the festivals and in Levitical circles of ancient Israel through hundreds of years. The concentric structural patterns, which are found at virtually all levels of analysis, bear witness to its tightly woven composition. That structure points to an author. On one level of observation that author is Moses, who composed the original Torah in musical form. But on another level the author is God himself, at work through a long chain of poet-prophets, like Moses, in ancient Israel who recited this text in public worship. Those poet-prophets made it the center of an elaborate canonical process that gave us the Bible itself as the Word of God.

Concept Check #23

What does the remark that Deuteronomy was in the hands of the Levites suggest about the transmission of this book in antiquity?

Check your answer at the back of this book.

C. Reading the Book of Deuteronomy from the Center

1. The Eleven Parashoth in the Book of Deuteronomy

Deuteronomy is structured in a concentric design in terms of eleven weekly portions in the annual cycle of Parashoth—the readings from the Torah in Jewish worship, as observed in synagogue tradition to the present day. These eleven readings may be outlined in a menorah pattern as follows:

---

12 T. Georgiades, *Music and Language: The Rise of Western Music as Exemplified in Settings of the Mass* (Cambridge: Cambridge University Press, 1982), 6.

The Eleven Parashoth in a Menorah Pattern	*Parashoth*	*Deut 1–34*
A Eisodus into Transjordan under Moses reviewed	# 44	1:1–3:22
B Essence of the covenant—Moses and the Ten Words	# 45	3:32–7:11
C Life in the Promised Land—the great peroration	# 46	7:12–11:25
X **Deuteronomic Code of Law**	# 47–49	11:26–25:19
C´ Public worship & covenant renewal in the Promised Land	# 50	26:1–29:9
B´ Appeal for covenant loyalty	# 51	29:10–30:20
A´ Eisodus into Cisjordan under Joshua anticipated	# 52–54	31:1–34:12

The most striking confirmation of this concentric design is found in the continuity between 3:22 and 31:1–3 in the outermost frame of this menorah pattern. The setting and content of these verses is the same, as Moses is turning over the leadership of Israel to his successor Joshua. There is no mention of Joshua in the book of Deuteronomy between these two passages.

The close connection between 11:26–32 and 27:1–8, both of which focus on the covenant blessings and curses on Mount Gerizim and Mount Ebal (near Shechem in Cisjordan), raises interesting questions; for the structural division in question does not correspond with the boundaries of the Parashoth. This matter is taken up in detail below, in the section on "The Numerical Composition of Deuteronomy."

1. Parashah 44 (Deut 1:1–3:22)
Eisodus into Transjordan under Moses

The first of the weekly portions in the public reading of Deuteronomy in Jewish worship (Parashah 44) may be outlined in a nested series of menorah patterns:

Parashah 44 : Debarim (Words)	*Deut 1:1–3:22*
A Summons to enter the Promised Land	1:1–8
B Organization of the people for life in the land	1:9–18
C Israel's unholy war—failure to enter the Promised Land	1:19–2:1
X **March of conquest from Mount Seir to the Promised Land**	2:2–25
C´ Yahweh's Holy War—conquest of Sihon and Og in Transjordan	2:26–3:11
B´ Distribution of the land in Transjordan	3:12–17
A´ Summons to take possession of the Promised Land	3:18–22

2ⁿᵈ Level Menorah: The March from Seir to the Promised Land	*Deut 2:2–25*
A Summons to journey northward (to the land beyond Edom)	2:2–3
B You are to pass through the territory of the children of Esau	2:4
C Summons not to contend with the children of Esau	2:5–6
X **A look back at what God has already done in Transjordan**	2:7–16
C´ Summons not to contend with the children of Lot (Moab and Ammon)	2:17–21
B´ The children of Esau dispossessed the Horites in times past	2:22
A´ Summons to cross the Arnon Valley and to battle against Sihon	2:23–25

3rd Level Menorah: A Look Back at What God has Already Done   *Deut 2:7–16*

A	A look backward: God's provision for 40 years in the wilderness	2:7
B	Travel notice—we went from Seir to the wilderness of Moab	2:8
C	Moab belongs to the sons of Lot (who dispossessed the Emim)	2:9
X	**Rephaim lived there in times past (Moab calls them Emim)**	2:10–11
C´	Seir belongs to the sons of Esau who dispossessed the Horites	2:12
B´	Travel notice—we crossed the Zered Valley	2:13–14a
A´	A look backward: a generation of warriors dead	2:14b–16

The wars of Yahweh are in two parts: the Exodus from Egypt and the Eisodus into the Promised Land. The Eisodus in turn is in two phases: the conquest of Transjordan under Moses and the conquest of Cisjordan (the so-called "West Bank") under Joshua. The focus of interest here is on the Eisodus under Moses, in anticipation of what is yet to come under Joshua. Phase one of the Eisodus begins with Yahweh's march of conquest from Mount Seir in Edom to Transjordan north of the Arnon Valley. As one moves more deeply into the concentric menorah patterns in Parashah 44 (Deut 1:1–3:22), it becomes increasingly clear that what has already been achieved by Edom, Moab and Ammon is considered to be part of the Eisodus in the broadest sense. These members of the extended family of God's people, as it were, have already dispossessed the Horites and the Emim in Transjordan. These former inhabitants of the land are considered to be among the Rephaim, who are as "tall as the Anakim"—i.e., a legendary race of giants.

2. Parashah 45 (Deut 3:23–7:11)
Essence of the Covenant—the Ten Words

The second of the weekly portions (Parashah 45) may be outlined in a menorah pattern within a menorah pattern:

Parashah 45 : Va-'ethannan (I pleaded)   *Deut 3:23–7:11*

A	Transition from Moses to Joshua—"crossing over"	3:23–29
B	Exhortation to keep the Torah—focus on Commandments 1 and 2	4:1–40
C	Transition and introduction to the Ten Words of the Torah	4:41–49
X	**Theophany and covenant at Horeb—giving of the Ten Words**	5:1–22
C´	God's desire is for us to fear him by keeping the Torah	5:23–6:3
B´	Sermonic elaboration of Commandments 1 and 2	6:4–25
A´	The practice of holiness in the land by keeping the Torah	7:1–11

2nd Level Menorah: Theophany and Covenant—the Ten Words   *Deut 5:1–22*

A	Yahweh's covenant and theophany	5:1–5
B	Monotheism—Commandments 1 through 3	5:6–11
C	Fourth Commandment: Observe the Sabbath	5:12–14
X	**Remember your deliverance from slavery in Egypt (Exodus)**	5:15
C´	Fifth Commandment: "Honor your father and your mother"	5:16
B´	Morality—Commandments 6 through 10	5:17–21
A´	Yahweh's theophany and covenant	5:22

The focus of attention here is on God's revelation to Moses on Mount Sinai and the covenant established at that time, which centers in the Ten Commandments (the Ten Words). The first four commandments deal with the vertical relationship between human beings and God in terms of the concept of monotheism and proper worship. The last six commandments deal with the horizontal relationship between human beings in terms of moral conduct:

A. Our Relationship to God (5:12–15):   1. No other gods allowed
                                          2. No images allowed
                                          3. No misuse of Yahweh's name allowed
                                          4. Observe the Sabbath
B. Our Relationship to Others (5:16–21)   5. Honor your father and your mother
                                          6. Do not kill
                                          7. Do not commit adultery
                                          8. Do not steal
                                          9. Do not bear false witness
                                          10. Do not covet what belongs to your neighbor

These commandments are the stipulations of the covenant relationship between God and his people.

God's desire for his people is explored further in a subsequent menorah pattern:

God's Desire Is that We Fear Him by Keeping the Torah	*Deut 5:23–6:3*
A Yahweh spoke to us on the mountain from the midst of the fire	5:23–24
B People address Moses: The fire will consume us, be out mediator	5:25–27
C Yahweh's speech: I hear what the people said	5:28
X **Would that they fear me by keeping my commandments**	5:29–30
C´ Yahweh's speech: Let me tell you the commandments	5:31
B´ Moses says to the people: Do what Yahweh has commanded	5:32–6:1
A´ That you may fear Yahweh by keeping his commandments	6:2–3

Within Parashah 45, the moral life that God demands is explored still further in another menorah pattern:

The Practice of Holiness in the Land by Keeping the Torah	*Deut 6:4–7:11*
A The great commandment: Love Yahweh your God	6:4–9
B Remember to fear Yahweh, for he is a jealous God	6:10–15
C Be careful to keep the commandments	6:16–19
X **Tell your children of the Exodus from Egypt**	6:20–22
C´ Yahweh will preserve us, if we keep his commandments	6:23–25
B´ Destroy your enemies, for you are a holy people	7:1–10
A´ Summary: Keep Yahweh's commandments	7:11

> ### Concept Check #24
> What is the "Principle Commandment" (the Great Command-ment) in the book of Deuteronomy?
> Check your answer at the back of this book.

3. Parashah 46 (Deut 7:12–11:25)
Conditional Blessing for Life in the Land

The third weekly portion (Parashah 46) in Deuteronomy may be outlined in a menorah pattern within a menorah pattern:

Parashah 46 : 'Ekev (Because)	*Deut 7:12–11:25*
A You will be blessed above all the peoples if you obey	7:12–26
B Remember the lessons from the wanderings in the wilderness	8:1–20
C Hear, O Israel, you are about to cross the Jordan River	9:1–29
X **At that time Yahweh spoke the Ten Words**	10:1–7
C´ At that time Yahweh set apart the tribe of Levi	10:8–11
B´ Love God and remember what he did for you in the wilderness	10:12–11:9
A´ If you love God, you will possess the Promised Land	11:10–25

2ⁿᵈ Level Menorah: At That Time Yahweh Spoke the Ten Words	*Deut 10:1–7*
A Moses is told to replace the stone tablets and make an ark to hold them	10:1
B God promises to write the words again on the tablets	10:2
C Moses makes the ark, takes the tablets and goes up the mountain	10:3
X **Yahweh writes the Ten Words and gives them to Moses**	10:4
C´ Moses goes down the mountain	10:5a
B´ Moses puts the tablets in the ark he has made	10:5b
A´ Israel journeys on, Aaron dies and is replaced by Eleazar	10:6–7

Once again, the focus of attention is on keeping the Ten Commandments that Moses receives from God on Mount Sinai. That point is reiterated within Parashah 46 in two more menorah patterns:

Love God and Remember What He Did for You in the Wilderness	*Deut 10:12–11:9*
A God requires that you love him by keeping his commandments	10:12–13
B God chose you and your children above all peoples	10:14–15
C Circumcise the foreskins of your hearts—love the resident alien	10:16–19
X **Love Yahweh your God by keeping his commandments**	10:20–11:1
C´ Your children do not know what God did in the Exodus	11:2–4
B´ Your eyes have seen what God did for you in the wilderness	11:5–7
A´ Keep the commandments that you may live in the land	11:8–9

If You Love God You Will Possess the Promised Land	*Deut 11:10–25*
A The land you are entering is not like the land of Egypt	11:10
B Yahweh is the one who takes care of the land your are entering	11:11–12
C If you obey these commandments, God will bless you in the land	11:13–15
X **Keep "these my words" before you; do not serve other gods**	11:16–19
C´ Keep these commandments before you and remain in the land	11:20–21
B´ If you keep this commandment Yahweh will drive the nations out	11:22–23
A´ All of the land on which your foot treads will be yours	11:24–25

4. Parashoth 47–49 (Deut 11:26–25:19) The Deuteronomic Code of Law

The laws of Israel's covenant with Yahweh in Parashot 47 through 49 (Deut 11:26–25:19) touch on virtually every aspect of a person's life in ancient Israel. On first glance, the contents appear to be arranged in a somewhat random order—particularly in Deuteronomy 19–25. The key to understanding the arrangement of these laws is to note that they appear in the order of the Ten Commandments of 5:6–21, and that they form a community or expansion of these summary laws, as follows:

Commandment			*Section in Deut 12–25*
Introduction		11:26–32	covenant renewal in convocation
1–2	no other gods but Yahweh	12:1–13:19	worship at the central sanctuary
3	taking God's name in vain	14:1–21	a holy people in relation to God
4	keeping the Sabbath holy	14:22–16:17	cult and society in sacred rhythm
5	parental respect	16:18–18:22	leadership and authority in Israel
6	homicide	19:1–21:9	murder, justice, and war
7	adultery	21:10–24:4	marriage, family, sex, and mixtures
8–10	theft, false testimony, and coveting	24:5–25:16	humanitarian concerns
Addendum		25:17–19	remember to hate the Amalekites

Another way of looking at the overall structure of what is often called the "Central Core" (Deut 12–26) is to outline its content in a menorah pattern:

The Deuteronomic Code of Law in Its Literary Context	*Deut 11:26–26:19*
A Covenant renewal in convocation	11:26–32
B Public worship at the central sanctuary and in local towns	12:1–14:21
C Laws on human affairs in relation to God	14:22–16:17
X **Laws on leadership and authority—executive and judicial**	16:18–21:9
C´ Laws on human affairs in relation to others	21:10–25:19
B´ Public worship at the central sanctuary and in local towns	26:1–15
A´ Mutual covenant commitments between Yahweh and Israel	26:16–19

a. Laws on Human Affairs in Relation to God (Deut 11:26–16:17)

The laws in Parashah 47 (Deut 11:26–16:17), which focus on human affairs in relation to God, may be outlined in a nested menorah pattern, as follows:

Parashah 47 : *Re'eh (See)*   *Deut 11:26–16:17*

A Covenant renewal under Moses in Moab and Joshua in Shechem   11:26–32
B   Laws that ensure exclusive worship of Yahweh—no idolatry   12:1–13:18
C   Do not gash yourself (blood implied), for you are a holy people   14:1–2
X   **What you may eat of land, water and winged animals**   14:3–21a
C´   You are holy; do not boil a kid in its mother's milk (blood implied)   14:21b
B´   Periodic duties—tithes, protection of the poor, firstborn   14:22–15:23
A´ Pilgrimage festivals to the central sanctuary in the Promised Land   16:1–17

2ⁿᵈ Level: What You May Eat of Land, Water and Winged Animals *Deut 14:3–21a*

A Do not eat any abominable thing   14:3
B   Land animals: eat those with divided hooves that chew the cud   14:4–6
C   Do not eat certain animals that merely appear to chew the cud   14:7
X   **Do not eat swine—it parts the hoof but does not chew the cud**   14:8
C´   Water animals: Eat only that which has fins and scales   14:9–10
B´   Winged animals: All clean birds and winged things you may eat   14:11–20
A´ Do not eat anything that dies of itself—give that to the resident alien   14:21a

The outermost frame in the concentric structure of Parashah 47 focuses on matters of worship at the central sanctuary in the Promised Land—in terms of covenant renewal at Shechem (11:26–32) and the three pilgrimage festivals to the central sanctuary (16:1–17). The second frame takes up the matter of idolatry and proper worship at the central sanctuary (12:1–13:18) and the periodic duties demanded of the worshiping community (14:22–15:23).

The innermost frame consists of two brief laws, both of which make implicit reference to illicit use of blood. On the one hand, we have the prohibition of pagan mourning customs that require drawing blood by gashing oneself (14:1–2); and, on the other hand, we have the peculiar prohibition of boiling a kid in its mother's milk (14:21b). This latter law is closely connected with the section at the center of this menorah pattern, which delineates what one may eat of land, water, and winged animals (14:3–21a). Jewish tradition has built the system of the kosher kitchen from this verse (cf. Exod 23:19; 34:26), in which meat and dairy products are kept separate—including the utensils and dishes used to cook and eat them. Casper Labuschagne calls attention to the fact that at eight days after the birth of the firstborn, the mother goat is still producing beestings, which are of a reddish color. As Labuschagne puts it, "Modern science has taught us that this is due to the high concentration of albumen and globulin, proteins which occur in blood, and owing to the fact that to a greater or lesser extent beestings do contain actual blood" (*The Scriptures and the Scrolls*, ed. F. García Martínez. VTSup 49 [Leiden: Brill, 1992], pp. 6–17). The concentric structure shown here supports this conclusion in drawing attention to the parallel text in 14:1–2, both of which make implicit reference to forbidden practices involving blood. The two passages serve as a framework to set off the detailed account of what one may eat of land, water, and winged animals in 14:3–21a.

At the structural center of this list we find the command not to eat swine (14:8), because that animal parts the hoof but does not chew the cud. Scholars continue to debate the reasoning behind this prohibition. Whatever the reason, the prohibition of eating pork is central in Jewish (and Muslim) cultures.

The two laws concerning illicit use of blood in this context (14:1–2 and 21b) call attention to the laws concerning sacred and secular slaughter in ancient Israel (12:8–28), which may be outlined in a menorah pattern, as follows:

Laws on Sacred and Secular Slaughter in Ancient Israel	*Deut 12:8–28*
A Worship Yahweh with your tithes and offerings at the central sanctuary	12:8–12
B *Take heed that you do not* offer sacrifices wherever you choose	12:13
C Offer sacrifices at the place God chooses	12:14a
X **Eat meat but pour out the blood on the ground**	12:14b–16
C′ Eat the tithe and offerings in the place God chooses	12:17–18
B′ *Take heed that you do not* forsake the Levite	12:19
A′ You may eat meat at home but not blood; pour out the blood properly	12:20–28

Proper disposal of the blood is absolutely essential and holiness itself is at stake. That's the issue in 14:21 when it makes the assertion that because "you are a people holy to Yahweh your God, 'You shall not boil a kid in its mother's milk.'" Life itself is in the blood (cf. Lev 17:11).

Concept Check #25

Why was it so important in ancient Israel to dispose of blood properly?

Check your answer at the back of this book.

---

b. Laws on Leadership—Judicial, Political and Priestly (Deut 16:18–21:9)

The laws on leadership in Parashah 48 (Deut 16:18–21:9) occupy the second level in a nested menorah pattern, which includes the whole of the so-called "Central Core" of Deuteronomy (12:1–26:19), as outlined above. The content of Parashah 48 may be outlined in a menorah pattern within a menorah pattern:

2ⁿᵈ Level Menorah—Parashah 48: Shofetim (Judges)	*16:18–21:9*
A You shall appoint judges and officials in your towns	16:18–20
B Do not erect an *asherah* or sacred pillar beside Yahweh's altar	16:21–22
C Do not sacrifice a blemished animal to Yahweh	17:1
X **Laws on leadership—judicial, political and priestly**	17:2–19:19
C′ *Lex talionis* is intended as a deterrent to false witnesses	19:20–21
B′ Humanitarian concerns: holy war—deferments and limits	20:1–20
A′ Unsolved murder—role of elders and judges	21:1–9

3rd Level: Laws on Leadership—Judicial, Political and Priestly *Deut 17:8–19:13*

A Law on idolatry within the gates of local towns in the land			17:2–7
B Law concerning the central tribunal						17:8–13
C Law of the king								17:14–20
X **Law of the Levites—endowment of the clergy**			18:1–8
C´ Law of the prophets							18:9–22
B´ Laws concerning the cities of asylum—manslaughter			19:1–13
A´ Laws on encroachment and witnesses in court				19:14–19

The laws in Parashoth 48 (16:18–21:9), which occupy the central position in the concentric structural design of Deuteronomy as a whole, focus attention on matters of leadership and authority in ancient Israel, namely on laws pertaining to judges, officials, the king, Levitical priests, prophets, and judicial courts. The fact that this reading is found at the second level in the nested menorah patterns shows that the Central Core (Deuteronomy 12–26) is carefully integrated into its larger literary context. This conclusion is substantiated by the observation that chapter 26 is in fact the first section of Parashah 50 (Deut 26:1–29:9).

As one moves more deeply into the nested menorah patterns at the center of Deuteronomy, the focus centers on laws concerning leadership and authority, both civic and religious. At the very center of Deuteronomy we find the brief law of the Levites (18:1–8), who were probably the ones responsible for the transmission of this legal corpus in ancient Israel. On either side of this law we find the pivotal laws on the king and the prophets, which play a dominant role in shaping the content of much of the Former Prophets—especially 1 and 2 Kings.

Concept Check #26

Explain how the law of the king in Deuteronomy (17:14–20) essentially forbids the king in ancient Israel to be king in the way that term is normally understood in the ancient Near East?

Check your answer at the back of this book.

---

c. Laws on Human Affairs in Relation to Others (Deut 21:10–25:19)

The forty-three laws in Parashot 49–50 (Deut 21:10–25:19), which focus on human affairs in relation to others, may also be outlined in a menorah pattern, as follows:

Parasha 49: Ki Tetse' (When you go out)			*Deut 21:10–25:19*

A On marriage—with a woman captured in war				21:10–14
B Twelve laws on family, "true religion," and illicit mixtures		21:15–22:12
C Six laws on sexual misconduct					22:13–29
X **Prohibition of marrying one's father's wife**			22:30
C´ Seven laws on "true religion"					23:1–25
B´ Fifteen laws on marriage, war, and "true religion"			24:1–25:16
A´ On war—remember to hate the Amalekites				25:17–19

Since there are eleven weekly portions in the cycle of Torah readings in Deuteronomy, Parashah 49 is also a structural center—the middle week in a sequence of eleven weeks. As such it illustrates the phenomenon of the "riddle in the middle" in a remarkable manner. In the center of this structure we find a curious law that prohibits a man from marrying his father's wife (22:30). This law functions as a literary bridge connecting two larger groups of laws on matters of social ethics (21:10–22:29 and 23:1–25). It is also parallel with a somewhat similar law prohibiting remarriage if one's former wife has remarried (24:1–4), which functions in the same manner connecting the laws of 23:1–25 and 24:5–25:19.

5. Parashah 50 (Deut 26:1–29:9)
Worship and Covenant Renewal in the Land

The content of Parashah 50 (Deut 26:1–29:9), which deals with matters of public worship and covenant renewal, may be outlined in a nested menorah pattern:

Parashah 50 : Ki Tavo' (When you come)	*Deut 26:1–29:9*
A Preview—two liturgies for worship in the Promised Land	26:1–15
B Mutual commitment between God and Israel in covenant renewal	26:16–19
C Shechem ceremony dramatizing Israel's covenant responsibilities	27:1–10
X Curses and blessings—with 3-fold expansion of curses	27:11–28:57
C´ Final curse: the complete reversal of Israel's history	28:58–68
B´ Summation: "These are the words of the covenant"	29:1
A´ Review—remembering the mighty acts of God in times past	29:2–9

2nd *Level Menorah: Covenant Curses and Blessings*	*Deut 27:11–28:57*
A Positioning of the tribes at Shechem and litany of curses	27:11–26
B Six covenant blessings (in three pairs)	28:1–6
C Promises expanding on the blessings	28:7–10
X Threefold blessing: progeny, property (livestock), and produce	28:11
C´ Promises expanding on the blessings	28:12–14
B´ Six covenant curses (in three pairs)	28:15–19
A´ Three-fold expansion of the covenant curses	28:20–57

The first half of the outermost frame in this menorah pattern, with its two liturgies for use in the annual pilgrimage festivals (26:1–15), functions as a transitional passage. It ties together the stipulations of the covenant as spelled out in the laws of the Central Core (Deut 12–26) with the covenant ceremony that follows in 27:1–29:9 and the appeal for covenant loyalty in 29:10–30:20.

A close reading of Deut 27–30 reveals a mixture of two covenant ceremonies: one on the plains of Moab, in the days of Moses, and another to be observed at Shechem under Joshua. The covenant ceremony that Moses commands Joshua to observe in the Promised Land may be outlined in a menorah pattern, as follows:

Ceremony Dramatizing Israel's Covenant Responsibilities   *Deut 27:1–10*

A   Moses' summary commandment   27:1
B   Write the Torah on plastered stones on Mount Ebal   27:2–4
C   Build there an altar of unhewn stones to Yahweh   27:5–6a
X   **Offer burnt offerings on it to Yahweh your God**   27:6b
C´   Sacrifice peace offerings and eat there—rejoice before Yahweh   27:7
B´   Write the Torah on plastered stones—very plainly   27:8
A´ Moses' pronouncement and summary commandment   27:9–10

Joshua subsequently did what Moses commanded him to do. "And there, in the presence of the people of Israel, he wrote upon stones a copy of the Torah of Moses . . . And afterward he read all the words of the Torah, the blessings and the curse, according to all that is written in the book of the Torah" (Josh 8:32–34). In recent years, Israeli archaeologists have located what appears to be Joshua's altar on Mount Ebal, which is reconstructed as follows:

The Altar Complex on Mount Ebal
(Source: Prof. Adam Zertal, *Biblical Archaeology Review* 11.1 [1985], p. 35)

It is useful here to anticipate the discussion to follow in Parashah 51 (29:10–30:20) by outlining the whole in a five-part concentric structure, as follows:

Parashoth 51–52: Worshipping in a Covenant Community   *Deuteronomy 26–30*

A   Public worship at the annual festivals in the Promised Land   Deut 26:1–19
B   The covenant blessings and curses   Deut 27:1–28:68
X   **Summation: "These are the words of the covenant"**   Deut 29:1
B´   The covenant is for future generations too   Deut 29:2–29
A´ The terms of the covenant are doable   Deut 30:1–20

The outermost frame opens with a brief summary of the nature of "true religion" in the Promised Land, in which the needs of "the Levite and the resident alien in your midst" are met (26:10–11). It concludes the assurance that "this commandment that I command you today is not too hard for you" (30:11). This instruction is not beyond reach, it is doable. The words of the covenant are the words that Yahweh commanded Moses in the land of Moab, in addition to the covenant he made with them at Mount Sinai (29:1). The movement in the inner frame of the above structure is from an expanded description of future disasters in the wake of covenant violation (28:20–37) to the declaration that the terms of the covenant apply for future generations as well (29:13–14).

As one moves more deeply into the center of the three-fold expansion of the curses at the structural center of the initial menorah pattern (27:11–28:57), we find in the center of the center a three-fold blessing: progeny, property (in terms of livestock), and produce (28:11). This theme is developed in numerous ways throughout the extensive section on the covenant curses and blessings in Deut 27–28, which is illustrated in the outline of the second expansion of the curses in a nested menorah pattern:

Second Expansion of Curses: Oppression, Exile and Slavery	*Deut 28:20–44*
A Triad of afflictions: curse, confusion, and cumbrance	28:20–22
B Agricultural disaster (drought and hardened soil)	28:23–24
C War: defeat leading to Israel becoming an object lesson	28:25–26
X **Physical and emotional oppression—undoing the blessing**	28:27–35
C´ War: exile leading to Israel becoming an object lesson	28:36–37
B´ Agricultural disaster (crop-destroying pests)	28:38–42
A´ Economic collapse—impoverishment and debt	28:43–44

2nd Level Menorah: Physical and Emotional Oppression	*Deut 28:27–35*
A "Boils" of Egypt (sent from Yahweh)	28:27
B Madness and blindness	28:28–29a
C Oppressed and robbed all the days	28:29b
X Undoing of the three-fold blessing (in 28:4, 8, 11)	28:30–31
C´ Oppressed and crushed all the days	28:32–33
B´ Madness from what one sees	28:34
A´ "Boils" (sent from Yahweh)	28:35

The detailed parallelism within this elaborate expansion of covenant curses has drawn comment from numerous scholars. The tedious listing of calamities displays unusual balance and symmetry, which converges on the undoing of the three-fold blessing that God has bestowed on his covenant people in progeny, property (livestock), and produce.

Concept Check #27

What took place on Mount Gerizim and Mount Ebal and what function does this have within the book of Deuteronomy?

Check your answer at the back of this book.

6. Parashah 51 (Deut 29:10–30:20): An Appeal for Covenant Loyalty

Parashah 51, the eighth of the eleven weekly portions in the annual cycle of Torah readings from Deuteronomy, is known as "Taking One's Stand," from its opening words in the Hebrew text. Individuals are invited to take their stand as obedient members of the covenant community. The covenant is intended not only for "those who are here with us standing today before Yahweh our God"; it is also "with those who are not here with us today" (29:15)—that is, for all future generations of God's people. The content of Parashah 51, which is an appeal for covenant loyalty, may be outlined in a menorah pattern, as follows:

Parashah 51 : Nitsavim (Standing)	*Deut 29:10–30:20*
A The covenant is binding on future generations too	29:10–15
B Those with reservations about keeping the covenant are warned	29:16–21
C Exile from the land foretold for breaking the covenant	29:22–28
X **Secret and revealed things: "Do all the words of this Torah"**	29:29
C′ Possibility of restoration—when you return, God will return	30:1–10
B′ God's commandments are doable	30:11–14
A′ The choice before you is between life and death—choose life	30:15–20

The center of this menorah pattern contains perhaps the most striking example of the principle of the "riddle in the middle" in the book of Deuteronomy. The words translated "to us and to our children" in 29:29 constitute the tenth (and final) example of the *Nequdoth* in the Torah. Each of the ten consonants of the Hebrew text has a special mark over it in the Leningrad Codex. The Aleppo Codex, however, has twelve dots rather than ten. These dots function as a form of commentary in shorthand, or homiletic notes to such a commentary, on the Hebrew text. The twelve dots in the Aleppo Codex may refer to the twelve tribes of Israel, which the scribe understood to be the meaning of the words "to us and to our children." The secret things belong to God; but God's revelation in "the words of this Torah" belongs to Israel. The ten dots in the Leningrad Codex may refer to the "Ten Words" (Ten Commandments), which are expanded into what eventually becomes the book of Deuteronomy as we now have it.

The scribe who added the *Nequdoth* was probably aware of the fact that the numerical value of the two words under the dots is 32 + 64 (= 2 x 32) = 96 (= 3 x 32). In terms of the usual association of the number 32 with the Hebrew word for "glory" כבוד (20 + 2 + 6 + 4 = 32), in the numerical composition of Deuteronomy, this number is used to call attention to the glory of Yahweh. It is probably no coincidence that the numerical value of the Hebrew word ישראל "Israel" is 64 (= 10 + 21 + 20 + 1 + 12). The glory of Israel is to be found in the Torah, which God entrusted to her (cf. Deut 4:5–8). The ten curious dots over ten successive letters in the Hebrew text stand for the "Ten Words," which are entrusted to Israel. And those words are "for us and for our children," that is, for all Israel. In short, Deuteronomy has the title "these are the words," which are in essence an expansion of the original "Ten Words" (the Ten Commandments). The secret things belong to God, but the revealed things belong to us and to our children forever—namely, "to do all the words of this Torah." The *Nequdoth*, at least in this instance, constitute a form of homiletical notes for the informed rabbi to teach the central message of Deuteronomy.

The "riddle in the middle" in 29:29 is followed immediately by a menorah pattern that reiterates the "great commandment," which plays such a prominent role in Parashah 45 (Deut 3:23–7:11; see especially 6:4–9).

Possibility of Restoration: When You Return, God will Return	*Deut 30:1–10*
A Recall these words and return to Yahweh	30:1–2
B Yahweh will restore you and he will return	30:3
C Yahweh will bring you back to the land of your fathers	30:4–5
X **Love Yahweh your God with all you heart and with all your soul**	30:6–7
C´ You will return and heed the voice of Yahweh	30:8
B´ Yahweh will return to take delight in you	30:9
A´ You will heed Yahweh's voice when you return to him	30:10

The key word שׁוב "return" appears in seven clauses within this menorah pattern. Three of these occurrences are in the outermost frame, which focuses on the need to return to Yahweh at that point in the future when the terms of the covenant have been broken (30:1–2). The way "to return" is to obey Yahweh's voice (30:10). The second frame also contains three occurrences of this key Hebrew verbal root in parallel verses (30:30 and 9), which focus on the assurance that Yahweh will *return* to his people and that he will *return* (i.e., restore) their fortunes after the captivity (30:3). The innermost frame has its focus on the fact that when the people *return* by obeying Yahweh (30:8), Yahweh will *return* them (bring them back) to the land of their fathers (30:4–5). And in the center we find a restatement of the "great commandment"—"to love Yahweh your God with all your heart and with all your soul" (30:6–7).

Concept Check #28

What are the Nequdoth in Deut 29:29?
Check your answer at the back of this book.

---

7. Parashoth 52–54 (Deut 31–34)
Anticipating the Eisodus into Cisjordan

The shift from the style of direct speech to that of narrative in Deut 31, and the disparate nature of its sub-units let Gerhard von Rad to conclude "that the material from chap. 31 onwards does not in any way belong to Deuteronomy any longer, but belongs instead to the great historical work in which Deuteronomy was aborted as a literary unit" (*Deuteronomy: A Commentary*. The Old Testament Library [Philadelphia: Westminster, 1966], p. 188). It was von Rad's failure to observe the concentric structure of the text that led to his negative assessment that "the whole chapter contains the debris of traditions rather than a real advance in the narrative" (p. 190). This chapter is in fact closely connected to 3:23–28 and plays a foundational role in the structure of all that follows in Deut 32–34. A different conclusion to that of von Rad is suggested by the following outline of 3:23–29 and 31:1–30 in menorah patterns:

Transition from Moses to Joshua: "Crossing Over"	*Deut 3:23–29*
A Introduction to the dialogue: Moses seeks God's favor	3:23
B Moses offers praise for the privilege of "seeing" God's greatness	3:24
C Moses asks permission to cross over to "see" the land	3:25
X **Yahweh is "cross" with Moses**	3:26
C´ Moses is permitted to "see" the land but not to cross over	3:27
B´ Moses is to command Joshua to cross over to the land Moses "sees"	3:28
A´ Concluding travel notice: "We remained opposite Beth-peor"	3:29

Moses' request for permission to "cross over" into Cisjordan (3:23–25) is set over against Yahweh's command that Moses encourage Joshua, who will "cross over before the people" (3:28). The center of this menorah pattern is marked by a whimsical sense of humor. Yahweh is "cross" with Moses in response to his request to "cross over" into Cisjordan (3:26). At the same time, Yahweh both denies and grants Moses' request to "see the good land that is beyond the Jordan" (3:25). Yahweh "did not listen" to Moses (3:26), and yet he did, for he commanded him to "go up to the top of the Pisgah (range) . . . and see with your eyes" (3:27). The transition in leadership from Moses to Joshua in 3:23–29 anticipates the commissioning of Joshua in 31:1–6. In a sense, the reader is invited to "cross over," as it were, to the other side of the book of Deuteronomy in terms of its concentric structural design—to Parashah 52 (Deut 31:1–30).

a. Appointment of Joshua and Disposition of the Torah (Deut 31:1–30)

In Deut 31–34 Moses obeys this command and he sees from the top of Mount Nebo what no tourist today can possibly see: "all the land, the Gilead as far as Dan, and all of Naphtali, and all the land of Ephraim and Manasseh, and all the land of Judah as far as the Western Sea, the Negev, and the Plain, that is, the valley of Jericho the city of palms, as far as Zoar" (34:1–3). In short, Moses "saw" all of the land, but he never set foot on any of it.

Parashah 52: Va-yelek (He went)	*Deut 31:1–30*
A Moses announces his departure and replacement by Joshua	31:1–6
B Moses appoints Joshua as his successor	31:7–8
C Torah to be read at the Feast of Booths to teach future generations	31:9–13
X **Theophany in the Meeting Tent with Moses and Joshua**	31:14–18
C´ The writing of the Song as a witness to future generations	31:19–22
B´ Yahweh appoints Joshua to succeed Moses	31:23
A´ The Torah and Song are given as witnesses to future generations	31:24–30

G. von Rad was correct in his assessment that Deut 31–34 is closely connected to the book of Joshua. It should be noted, however, how closely the center of the menorah pattern in 31:14–15 is related to a more distant text in Exod 33:11, which places Moses and Joshua together in the Meeting Tent. That text adds the note that Moses' servant Joshua "did not depart from the tent." The larger concentric design of the whole of the Primary History, in which this verse stands in the structural center of Exodus 33, is explored above in the section on "The Book of Exodus."

The final three weekly portions of Torah readings (Deut 31–34), which are read in the month of Tishri from Rosh Hashanah (1 Tishri) to *Simchat Torah* (23 Tishri), are shorter than the others, as the worshiping community moves into the high holy days of the Jewish calendar. The Ten Days of Repentance extend from Rosh Hashanah (1 Tishri) to Yom Kippur (Day of Atonement, 10 Tishri). The Festival of Booths (15–22 Tishri) follows them, which sets the stage for *Simchat Torah*—the end of the cycle of readings from the Torah and the beginning of the next.

The content of Parashoth 52–54 (Deut 31–34) may be outlined in nested menorah patterns in two different ways, depending on whether the focus of attention is on the Song of Moses (Deut 32) or the Testamentary Blessing of Moses (Deut 33). When the Song of Moses is the focus, the nested menorah pattern is as follows:

Parashoth 52–54: Anticipating the Eisodus into Cisjordan   *Deut 31:1–34:12*

A	Moses' final provisions in view of his impending death	31:1–13
B	Yahweh's charge to Moses and Joshua in the Meeting Tent	31:14–23
C	Moses gives the Torah to the Levitical priests	31:24–27
X	**The Song of Moses within its narrative context**	31:28–32:45
C´	Moses commands the people to observe the Torah	32:46–47
B´	Yahweh commands Moses to climb Mount Nebo to "see" the land	32:48–52
A´	Moses' blessing, death, funeral and necrology	33:1–34:12

2nd Level Menorah: The Song of Moses in its Narrative Context   *Deut 31:28–32:45*

A	Moses gathers the leaders to hear *the Song*	31:28–30
B	Yahweh's blessing of Israel in times past	32:1–14
C	Israel's disloyalty—they forsook the one who made them	32:15–18
X	**Yahweh's decision to punish Israel**	32:19–35
C´	Yahweh's loyalty—his plan to deliver Israel	32:36
B´	Yahweh's "vengeance"—punishment and salvation in the future	32:37–43
A´	Moses speaks all the words of *this Song* to the people	32:44–45

In this reading, the focus narrows to the issue of Yahweh's "vengeance"—his redemptive judgment on Israel. Yahweh himself decides to punish Israel for her disloyalty (32:19–35). But his anger has limits and he also shows mercy. He "redeems" the very people he "sold" (32:26–29).

b. Parashah 53 (Deut 32:1–52): *Ha' azinu* (Hear)—Song of Moses

The Song of Moses, which makes up the greater part of Parashah 53 (Deut 32:1–52), may be outlined in a nested menorah pattern of its own, as follows:

The Song of Moses   *Deut 32:1–43*
A Exordium: Yahweh's faithfulness and Israel's disloyalty   32:1–6
B   Past: Yahweh's benefactions to Israel in times past   32:7–14
C   Israel's disloyalty—they forsook the one who made them   32:15–18
X   **Yahweh's decision to punish Israel**   32:19–35
C´   Yahweh's loyalty—his plan to deliver Israel   32:36
B´   Future: Yahweh will take vengeance on his enemies   32:37–42
A´ Coda: Celebration of Yahweh's deliverance of Israel   32:43

2ⁿᵈ Level Menorah: Yahweh's Decision to Punish Israel   *Deut 32:19–35*
A Yahweh's response: "I will hide my face from them"   32:19–21
B   The fire of Yahweh's anger will consume the earth   32:22
C   Yahweh's judgment: bereavement and terror—for everyone   32:23–25
X   **Yahweh's mercy: he chooses to limit Israel's punishment** 32:26–29
C´   Our God is not like other gods—he "sold" Israel   32:30–31
B´   The enemy will drink the cup of Yahweh's wrath   32:32–33
A´ Yahweh's decision: "To me belongs vengeance and recompense"   32:34–35

In his study of the structure of the Song of Moses, Patrick Skehan argues persuasively that the poem as a whole divides naturally into three major parts (vv 1–14, 15–29, and 30–43). Each of these three parts has twenty-three versets. The structure observed by Skehan is confirmed on more objective grounds in my commentary on Deuteronomy. That structure is more complex than Skehan realized, however, as shown by noting the major divisions within the first and third sections:

The Song of Moses in a Five-Part Concentric Structure   *Deut 32:1–43*
A God's justice and Israel's disloyalty   32:1–6
B   God's blessing on Israel in times past   32:7–14
X   **Israel's sin provokes God's punishment**   32:15–29
B´   God's decision to punish both Israel and her enemies   32:30–35
A´ God's "vengeance"—Israel is delivered   32:36–43

In this reading there are 23 versets in the center section (32:15–29), and 23 versets in each of the two frames around that center: 32:1–6 + 36–43 and 32:7–14 + 30–35. There are also 23 versets in each of the three major parts of the Song of Moses (32:1–14, 15–29 and 30–43). In the numerical composition of the book of Deuteronomy, the number 23 is associated with the word "glory," which indicates that this remarkable poem was written to the glory of Yahweh.

c. Parashah 54 (Deut 33–34): *Vezo' t Ha-berakha* (This is the blessing)

The primary message of Parashoth 52–54 (Deut 31–34) shifts when the focus of attention moves to the Testamentary Blessing in chapter 33, as the following nested menorah pattern shows:

Parashoth 52–54: Anticipating the Eisodus into the Cisjordan   *Deut 31:1–34:12*
A   Moses' final charge to Joshua and to all Israel (and the Song)   31:1–32:47
B   Moses is commanded to ascend Mount Nebo to "see" the land   32:48–52
C   First stanza of ancient hymn: Yahweh's protection and provision   33:1–5
X   **Moses' testamentary blessing on the twelve tribes of Israel**   33:6–25
C´   Second stanza of ancient hymn: Israel's security and blessing   33:26–29
B´   Moses ascends Mount Nebo where he "sees" the Promised Land   34:1–4
A´ Transition of leadership from Moses to Joshua   34:5–12

2nd **Level Menorah: Testamentary Blessing on the Twelve Tribes**   *Deut 33:6–25*
A   Reuben and Judah   33:6–7
B   Levi—with the first apostrophe (and Simeon?)   33:8–11
C   Benjamin   33:12
X   **Joseph (Ephraim and Manasseh)**   33:13–17
C´   Zebulun and Issachar   33:18–19
B´   Gad—with the second apostrophe   33:20–21
A´ Dan, Naphtali, and Asher   33:22–25

The outermost frame in this menorah pattern moves from Moses' final charges to Joshua and the people of Israel (31:1–32:47) to the transition of leadership from Moses to Joshua (34:5–12). The words of 32:48–52, which look back to 3:27 and even further back to Num 27:12–14, are now fulfilled explicitly in 34:1–4 as Moses ascends Mount Nebo to "see" the Promised Land. Two stanzas of an ancient hymn of praise to Yahweh are used as the innermost frame to highlight the blessings bestowed on the tribes of Israel (33:6–25). As we move more deeply into the center itself, the focus narrows to the tribe of Joseph (i.e., Ephraim and Manasseh).

At this point, it is useful to call the reader's attention to the earlier discussion of "Genesis 1–11 as Introduction to the Bible." Parashoth 54 (Deut 33–34), the final reading in the annual cycle of Torah readings, takes place on *Simchat Torah*, the 23rd of Tishri. The concluding section of this reading may be outlined as follows:

A   Moses saw the whole of the land "with his *eyes*"   34:1–4
B   Death and burial of Moses—"no one *knows* where"   34:5–6
X   **Moses was 120 years old—"his *eye* was not dim"**   34:7–8
B´   Incomparability of Moses—"whom Yahweh *knew* face to face"   34:9–10
A´ Moses did great wonders "before *the eyes* of all Israel"   34:11–12

The first weekly portion (Gen 1:1–6:8), which is known as "In the beginning," commences on *Simchat Torah*, when the Torah scroll is re-rolled to its beginning. The second portion (Gen 6:9–11:32) is known as "Noah." When the content of these two readings is outlined in a menorah pattern, we have the following:

Parashoth 1 and 2 in a Menorah Pattern	*Genesis 1–11*
A Story of creation/dispersion [ending with three sons of Adam]	1:1–4:26
B Enoch (who "walked with God")	5:1–32
C Sons of God take daughters of *ha'adam* as wives	6:1–2
X Yahweh says: "he is flesh and his days shall be 120 years"	6:3
C´ Sons of God and daughters of *ha'adam* breed giants in the land	6:4
B´ Noah (who "walked with God"	6:5–9:29
A´ Story of dispersion [beginning with three sons of Noah]	10:1–11:32

The center of this structure presents the phenomenon of the "riddle in the middle," as the hearer is startled by the sudden reference to what looks at first glance like what is normally called mythology. The "sons of God" marry "daughters of Adam" to produce the giants of old (the *Nephilim*). In addition to the two interpretations of the curious word *beshaggam* in the center of the center in this menorah pattern discussed above, a third reading is also possible. More than a century ago, Abraham Geiger cited both Josephus and Jerome in his arguments that the word *beshaggam* refers to Moses in terms of gematria—where the words משה ("Moses") and בשגם (*beshaggam*) are identical. Moreover, in the regular cycle of weekly readings from the Torah, the text of Deut 34:7 is read the week before—on *Simchat Torah* (which translates as "the joy of the Torah").

Concept Check #29

What is unique about the death of Moses according to Deuteronomy?

Check your answer at the back of this book.

D. The Numerical Composition of Deuteronomy

Much has been written through the years on what Casper Labuschagne describes as "the misuse of numbers by numerologists,"[13] including the writings of Ivan Panin, K. G. Sabiers (*Astonishing New Discoveries: Thousands of Amazing Facts Discovered beneath the Very Surface of the Bible Text*), Friedrich Weinreb, and more recently M. Katz, F. Weiner, D. Ordman, and M. Drosnin (*The Bible Code* [New York: Simon & Schuster, 1997]). In spite of these excesses, which have done much to discredit serious academic research in this area, Labuschagne demonstrates that the pioneer work of C. Schedl laid the foundation for fruitful study of the composition, structure, and meaning of the biblical text as a numerical composition.

The first attempt in modern times to draw attention to the numerical aspects of the Hebrew Bible was made by Oskar Goldberg, who published his conclusions in 1908. On the first page of that work he states:[14]

---

13   C. J. Labuschagne, *Numerical Secrets of the Bible: Rediscovering the Bible Codes* (North Richland Hills, TX: BIBAL Press, 2000), 153-157.

14   The citation and translation here of Goldberg are taken from C. J. Labuschagne, *Numerical Secrets* (BIBAL Press, 2000), 111.

> The Pentateuch is from the beginning to the end a numerical system, whose basic numbers derive from the divine Name YHWH. This numerical system presents itself primarily in the contents of the text and subsequently in its style up to its most refined finesses, in fact in the entire architecture of the text divided into paragraphs, verses and parts of verses. It governs the words, determines the number of letters and becomes manifest in their numerical value as well, while the combination of these factors exhibits the fixed principle of one single number. Therefore the Pentateuch should be regarded as the unfolding of this basic number, as the Name YHWH being unfolded in a writing-in-numbers.

Goldberg argued his case in terms of specific texts, such as that of the genealogy of Shem in Gen 10:21–32. In the eleven verses of this passage, he observed that there are 104 (= 4 x 26) words, a multiple of the divine Name number 26. Moreover, he counts a total of 390 (= 15 x 26) letters in this passage, and he observes that there are a total of 26 descendants of Shem. He computes the numerical value of their names and finds that the first 13 names total 3,588 (= 138 x 26), while the names of the 13 sons of Joktan add up to 2,756 (= 106 x 26).

In the account of the war against Amalek in Exod 17:8–16, Goldberg counts a total of 119 (= 7 x 17) words, which is a multiple of the second divine Name number 17. The number of letters in this passage come to 449, which is not a multiple of 17, but the sum of the digits (4 + 4 +9) adds up to 17. Numerous other examples are presented that demonstrate the use of the numbers 7, 17 and 26 throughout the Torah in a manner that substantiates Goldberg's thesis that the Torah is a numerical composition governed by the number 7 and the two divine Name numbers 17 and 26.

Goldberg's work lay virtually ignored for more than half a century until it was picked up in the pioneering work of Claus Schedl, which itself set the stage for Casper Labuschagne's contribution. Numerical criticism, as a new perspective for traditional literary criticism of the biblical text, emerged when Schedl initiated what he calls logotechnical analysis (*logotechnique*). Schedl's work is grounded in three principles that are deeply embedded in Jewish tradition: 1) the letters of the Hebrew alphabet have numerical values (gematria); 2) a close relationship exists between counting and writing; and 3) a close relationship exists between the biblical texts and counting. Schedl's colleagues rejected his approach and he was hampered by the lack of a consulting partner (other than his own students at the University of Graz in Austria). Nevertheless, he groped his way alone in uncharted waters to lay the preliminary foundation on which Labuschagne would subsequently build a significant structure. Even so, the larger work of numerical structural analysis of biblical texts remains a task for others to complete in the years ahead. As a methodological principle, logotechnical analysis of the biblical text is still in its infancy.

Schedl studied the work of early Jewish mysticism, where he learned of "32 secret paths of wisdom" consisting of the "10 *Sefirot*" and the "22 elemental letters," which gave him the first significant formula for building biblical texts: 22 + 10 = 32. Other formulas followed, including what he calls the "minor tetraktys," in which a text has 55 words with one component of 23 words and the other of 32. The term "tetraktys" comes form the Pythagorean geometrical figure formed by the first *four* letters (numbers): 1, as a *point*; 2, as a *line*; 3, as a *triangle*; and 4 as a three-sided *pyramid*. The sum of these four numbers is 10 (1 + 2 + 3 + 4), the *decade*. The number 55 is the triangular number of 10, or the sum of 1 through 10. Schedl found that these numbers are arranged in the Babylonian and Pythagorean mathematical systems in such a way that they constitute a one-dimensional equilateral triangle, or a three-dimensional pyramid. This same geometrical form is the basis of speculation in Jewish mysticism concerning the letters of the tetragrammaton YHWH.

The fact that Deut 12:1–26:19 is read by many as a literary unit, when neither boundary corresponds with the boundaries of the weekly portions (Parashoth) in the annual cycle of Torah readings in Jewish worship, suggests that the cycle of weekly readings is imposed on an earlier structure. The Central Core belongs to that structure, which constitutes the center of a five-part structural design of Deuteronomy as a whole, namely "four wheels of the same likeness with a wheel within the four wheels":

A	1st Wheel—a look backward to the Eisodus (part one) under Moses	Deut 1–3
B	2nd Wheel—the great peroration (preaching of the covenant)	Deut 4–11
X	Central Core: the covenant stipulations	Deut 12–26
B′	3rd Wheel—the covenant ceremony	Deut 27–30
A′	4th Wheel—a look forward to Eisodus (part two) under Joshua	Deut 31–34

There is further evidence to support the conclusion that the Central Core in Deut 12–26 is a structural unit in the center of Deuteronomy as a whole, even though neither of the boundaries here corresponds to those of the Parashoth. Casper Labuschagne divides Deut 12–26 into ten sections, which are based on the order of the Ten Commandments, as follows:

I	12:1–13:19	1st and 2nd commandments	50 verses
II	14:1–21	3rd commandment	21 verses
III	14:22–16:17	4th commandment	48 verses
IV	16:18–18:22	5th commandment	47 verses
V	19:1–21:9	6th commandment	50 verses
VI	21:10–22:12	6th commandment	26 verses
VII	22:13–29	7th commandment	17 verses
VIII	23:1–26	6th–10th commandments	26 verses
IX	24:1–25:4	6th–10th commandments	26 verses
X	25:5–26:19	6th–10th commandments	34 verses

Labuschagne notes that the total number of verses in 12:1–16:17 is 119, which is what he calls a "holy number"—17 x 7.[15] The total number of verses in 16:18–22:29 is 140, which is the sum of the squares of the numbers one through seven. And the number of verses in 23:1–26:19 is 86 = 2 x (17 + 26). When the whole of Deut 12–26 is examined in detail, it is interesting to note that 12:1 and 26:16 function as an inclusion. The Central Core opens with the words, "These are the statutes and the judgments, which you shall be careful to do in the land" (12:1). It concludes with the words, "This day Yahweh

---

15 *De Prediking van het Oude Testament*, vol. II (Nijkerk: Uitgeverij G. F. Callenbach, 1990), pp. 12-14.

your God is commanding you to do these statutes and judgments; and you shall be careful to do them with all your heart and with all your soul" (26:16). Sandwiched between these two verses, as a structural frame, we find a total of exactly 340 (= 2 x 10 x 17) verses. The manner in which the numbers 7, 10, 17 and 26 are used to shape the literary structure of the Central Core in the book of Deuteronomy is indeed remarkable.

It is of particular interest to note the similarity between the words "YHWH" and "glory" in terms of their numerical value in the Hebrew language. Both words are interpreted as having the value of both 17 and 26, as Labuschagne has shown:

כבד, "glory"
alphabetical value: (כ = 11) + (ב = 2) + (ד = 4) = 17
as numerical signs: (כ = 20) + (ב = 2) + (ד = 4) = 26

יהוה, "YHWH"
alphabetical value: (י = 10) + (ה = 5) + (ו = 6) + (ה = 5) = 26
sum of digits: (י = 1 + 0 = 1) + (ה = 5) + (ו = 6) + (ה = 5) = 17

Labuschagne suggests that the number 17 may be associated with God's personal name in terms of the numerical value of אהוה *'ahweh*, which is analogous to the archaized form *yahweh* יהוה. The normal first person singular form אהיה *'ehyeh* occurs in the famous verse in Exod 3:14, where the divine name is revealed and defined—"I AM WHO I AM." The numerical value of אהוה is 17.

It is thus possible to read the combination of 17 + 26 = 43 as representing the "glory of YHWH" as well as the combination of the two divine-name numbers. Labuschagne discusses an alternate spelling of the word "glory" (כבד), sometimes written as כבוד in the Hebrew Bible, which he explains as follows:

alphabetical value: (כ = 11) + (ב = 2) + (ו = 6) + (ד = 4) = 23
value as numerical signs: (כ = 20) + (ב = 2) + (ו = 6) + (ד = 4) = 32

Labuschagne finds numerous examples of the combination of these two numbers in Deuteronomy in the pattern 23+32 = 55 (the "minor tetraktys"). He also calls attention to other ways to represent the "glory of YHWH" (כבוד יהוה): (23+17) = 40; (23+26) = (32+17) = 49 (= 7^2); and (32+26) = 58.

To understand how the sacred numbers are used in the final composition of the Hebrew text of Deuteronomy, one must know that most verses in the Hebrew Bible are divided into two parts by the presence of an accent marker known as the *'atnach*. The counting of words within a given text to achieve a numerical multiple of 17 and 26 applies not only to the total number of words in a given text, but also to the number of words before *'atnach* or after *'atnach* in that text.

Surprising conclusions emerge in the grand totals for extended passages in Deuteronomy, particularly in the eleven weekly portions (Parashoth) of the annual cycle of Torah readings. The use of the two divine-name numbers (17 and 26) and the number 23 (the numerical value of the word "glory"), in terms of the total word-count within the eleven Parashoth in Deuteronomy, may be summarized as follows:

Parashot		Words: before 'atnach	after 'atnach	Total Number of Words
44	1:1–3:22	860 (= 20x43)	+ 687	= 1,547 (= 91x17)
45	3:23–7:11	1,040	+ 833 (= 49x17)	= 1,873
46	7:12–11:25	927	+ 824	= 1,751 (= 103x17)
47	11:26–16:17	1,118 (= 43x26)	+ 814	= 1,932
48	16:18–21:9	867 (= 3x17x17)	+ 656	= 1,523
49	21:10–25:19	929	+ 652	= 1,581 (= 93x17)
50	26:1–19	183	+ 136 (= 8x17)	= 319
	27:1–29:8	841	+ 587	= 1,428 (= 84x17)
51	29:9–30:20	357 (= 21x17)	+ 306 (= 18x17)	= 663 (= 39x17)
52	31:1–30	322 (= 14x23)	+ 230 (= 10x23)	= 552 (= 24x23)
53	32:1–52	332	+ 289 (= 17x17)	= 621
54	33:1–34:12	301	+ 209	= 510 (= 30x17)
	11:26–26:19	3,097	+ 2,258	= 5,355 (= 315x17)
	31:1–34:12	955	+ 728 (= 28x26)	= 1,683 (= 99x17)
	33:2–25	301	+ 209	= 510 (= 30x17)
	1:1–34:12	8,077	+ 6,223	= 14,300 (= 55x10 x26)

In terms of word count, multiples of the numbers 17, 23, 26 and 43 (= 17 + 26) appear in all eleven of the Parashot in Deuteronomy, and in various larger combinations and subdivisions of these literary units. Moreover, the total number of words in Deuteronomy as a whole is a multiple of the divine-name number 26. The grand total of 14,300 words in the book of Deuteronomy is then a coded message about the book itself, which bears the title "These are the Words" with particular interest in the "Ten Words" (i.e., the Ten Commandments"). As the "minor tetraktys," the number 55 is the sum of the digits one through ten. The number 55 is multiplied by ten, which in turn is multiplied by the divine-name number 26, to obtain the total number of words in a book that bears the title, "These are the words (of Yahweh)."

Concept Check #30

How do you explain the data about the numerical composition of Deuteronomy?

Check your answer at the back of this book.

E. Law and Narrative in the Bible

David Daube and Calum Carmichael have demonstrated a close connection between
individual laws in Deuteronomy 12–25 and the language and literary structure of various narratives throughout the Torah and the Former Prophets. Arguing within the context of their professions as lawyers, Daube and Carmichael conclude that the compilers
studied existing biblical narrative and wrote selected laws in the form of legal abstracts.
My own study of the laws in Deuteronomy suggests that the process is complex and that,
for the most part, the direction of influence is in the opposite direction—the laws are
used to shape the narratives.

The canonical process begins with the Ten Commandments, which are used to
shape the content of the laws in Deuteronomy 12–26 (the so-called Central Core, or the
Deuteronomic Code of Law). The legislation here touches on virtually every aspect of a
person's life in ancient Israel, on both a community and an individual level. On first
glance, the contents appear to be arranged in a somewhat random order. The key to
understanding the arrangement of these laws is to note that they appear in the order of
the Ten Commandments (Deut 5:6–21), and that they form a commentary or expansion
of these summary laws.

Calum Carmichael has demonstrated a close connection between the wording of the
law in 22:30 and the narrative concerning Reuben and his father's concubine in Gen
35:22 and 49:4. The law prohibiting a man from taking his father's wife includes the
taking and possessing of his father's concubine. In other words, the law shapes the narrative, which focuses on Reuben's intercourse with Bilhah. In his discussion of what he calls
the law on "a forbidden relationship with a father's wife," Carmichael says: "In the law, a
man's wife is his skirt, and for a son to lie with her means that figuratively he has removed
his father's covering and put it on himself. In a literal sense he uncovers his stepmother's
nakedness, in a figurative sense, his father's" (*Law and Narrative in the Bible* [Ithaca: Cornell University Press, 1985], p. 222). This observation raises the question of the nature of
the whole of Parashah 49 (Deut 21:10–25:19), in particular, to narrative tradition in the
book of Genesis. It appears that we have here the most extensive occurrence of the phenomenon of the "riddle in the middle" within a concentric literary structure of the
Tanakh. A detailed discussion of this matter is beyond the scope of this introductory textbook. For purposes of illustration, a significant part of the data may be summarized in the
following nested menorah pattern:

Laws that Shape Narratives in Genesis, Exodus and Numbers		*Deut 24:5–25:19*
A Isaac and Ishmael: millstone as pledge	Gen 21:9–12	Deut 24:5–6
B Sale of Joseph: theft of a fellow Israelite	Gen 37:26–28	Deut 24:7
C Miriam's leprosy: dealing with "leprosy"	Num 12:1–14	Deut 24:8–9
X **Stories of the Fathers in Genesis**	Gen 15–38	Deut 24:10–25:10
C′ Judah and Tamar: immodest lady wrestler	Gen 38	Deut 25:11–12
B′ Joseph: honest weights and measures	Gen 42–44	Deut 25:13–16
A′ Amalek's attack: "remember to hate Amalek"	Exod 17:1–14	Deut 25:17–19

2nd Level: Stories of Abraham, Isaac, Jacob, Joseph and Judah   *Deut 24:10–25:10*

A	Finding a wife for Isaac: distrained property	Gen 24 (& 15)	Deut 24:10–13
B	Jacob and Laban: the hired servant	Gen 31:4–42	Deut 24:14–15
C	Hamor and his son Shechem: fathers & sons	Gen 34	Deut 24:16
X	Joseph: protecting the vulnerable	Gen 37–47	Deut 24:17–22
C´	Joseph in Egypt: limits on flogging	Gen 37–47	Deut 25:1–3
B´	Judah and Tamar: unmuzzling the ox	Gen 38	Deut 25:4
A´	Judah and Tamar: levirate marriage	Gen 38	Deut 25:5–10

It is useful at this point to examine specific laws in Parashah 49 (Deut 21:10–25:19) in relation to the corresponding narratives in Genesis to illustrate the process.

Similarity in the traditional titles of Parashah 7 (Gen 28:10–32:3) and Parashah 49 (Deut 21:10–25:19) suggest the possibility of a literary relationship between the two. The title of Parashah 7 is *Va-Yetse'* ("He went out") and the title of Parashah 49 is *Ki Tetse'* ("When you go out"). The same Hebrew verb appears in both titles. Moreover, the number of the two weekly portions in the annual cycle of readings from the Torah are closely related sacred numbers: 49 = 7 x 7.

Carmichael argues for literary dependence of the law on marriage with a woman captured in war in Deut 21:10–14 on the narrative about Jacob and Rachel in Gen 31:25–32, 48–50.[16] It is likely, however, that the order is the reverse of Carmichael's premise, namely that the narrative is shaped by the specific wording of the law in question.

The specific relationship between the laws in Deuteronomy and the narrative tradition in Genesis is seen most clearly in the case of the law on taking and holding distrained property in Deut 24:10–13, which may be translated as follows:

> When you make a loan to your neighbor, a loan of any sort,
>> you shall not enter his house to take his pledge—outside you shall stand.
> And the man to whom you make the loan shall bring to you the pledge outside.
> And if he is a poor man, you shall not sleep in his pledge.
> You shall surely return the pledge to him when the sun goes down,
>> that he may sleep in his garment and he shall bless you.
> And it shall be counted as righteousness for you before Yahweh your God.

Carmichael fails to note the relationship between the law in Deut 24:10–13 and the narratives in Genesis 15 and 24 precisely because of his presupposition regarding the direction of literary influence.

The law in Deut 24:10–13 is used to shape the story of Isaac in Genesis 24, where the "pledge" (*'abot*) is Rebekah, who is obtained by an unnamed servant sent to obtain the "pledge from the house of Laban." Specific wording in this story carries the reader back to an earlier story of Abram in Genesis 15, when God "brought him outside" and blessed him. Then, "as the sun was going down" . . . "when the sun had gone down . . . on that day Yahweh made a covenant with Abram" (Gen 15:12–18). Here Rebekah, the *'abot* in Genesis 24, is related to the "fathers" (*'abot*) of Genesis 15:15 in that she, like Sarai before her, is a "Matriarch"—one of the "mothers of the Fathers," as it were. Her descendants, through

---

16 C. Carmichael, *Law and Narrative in the Bible* (Cornell University Press, 1985), pp. 139-142.

her son Esau, include the chiefs of Edom, one of whom takes center stage in another time and another place within the biblical narrative—in the land of Uz. There, outside the house of Jacob, Job lives to see "his sons, and his son's sons, four generations." Like his "brother" Abram, Job dies, "an old man, and full of days" (Job 42:16–17, cf. Gen 15:15).

The words in the law "that he may sleep in his garment" (24:13) take on fresh meaning in relation to the story in Genesis, where Isaac "took Rebekah and she became his wife" (Gen 24:67). In the Hebrew text, this same expression appears in Deut 21:11; 22:13; 23:1 and 24:1–5 (five times). Moreover, the words "he shall bless you" (Deut 24:13) become "and they blessed" in Gen 24:60. They introduce the blessing pronounced by the men of Laban's house on Rebekah: "Our sister, may you become the mother of thousands of ten thousands, and may your descendants possess the gate of those who hate them!"

At this point, the reader is reminded of a similar blessing to Abraham in times past. And the very next phrase in the law of Deut 24:13, "it shall be counted as righteousness," takes us back to the narrative of God's covenant with Abram in Genesis 15. God *brought him outside* and said, "Look toward heaven and number the stars, if you are able . . . so shall your descendants be" (Gen 15:5). And Abram believed God, who *reckoned it to him as righteousness* (Gen 15:6). A bit later in the narrative, "Yahweh said to Abram, 'Know of a surety that your descendants will be . . . oppressed for four hundred years . . . As for yourself, you shall go to your fathers in peace; you shall be buried in a good old age. And *they shall come back here in the fourth generation*'" (Gen 15:12–18). This statement takes on new meaning in this reading, for that is what we just did in this reading of Genesis through the lens of the laws of Deuteronomy. The four generations are Abraham, Isaac, Jacob/Israel, and Jacob's twelve sons (the tribes of Israel), with the focus narrowing to the persons of Joseph (Deut 24:7, 17–22; 25:1–3, 13–16) and Judah (25:4–12) in that fourth generation. The moment the sale of Joseph by his brothers is first introduced in Deut 24:7 (in the law prohibiting a "theft" of a fellow Israelite) our attention is directed to Miriam's "leprosy" (Deut 24:8–9) in the era of the Exodus from Egypt. This is the "present," from the perspective of Deuteronomy. The next law (24:10–13) takes us back three generations to Isaac's quest for a wife in Gen 24:1–67, which then takes us back still further, one more generation, to the original story of Abram. There the author already outlined all that was to follow in a brief prophecy, which concludes with the curious words "they will come back here in the fourth generation."

In the next book of this series, we will examine in greater detail the law of the king (Deut 17:14–20) and the law of the prophets (18:9–22) in relation to the shaping of the narrative in the Former Prophets (Joshua through 2 Kings).

The Pentateuchal Structure of the Book of Deuteronomy

[Four Wheels of the Same Likeness and a Wheel within the Four Wheels]

A	*Looking Back to the Exodus from Egypt*	*Deut 1–3*
a	Summons to enter the Promised Land	1:1–8
b	Organization of the people for life in the land	1:9–18
x	The wars of Yahweh—phase one: conquest of the Amorite kings	1:19–3:11
b´	Distribution of the land in Transjordan	3:12–17
a´	Summons to take the Promised Land	3:18–22
B	*Preparation for the Covenant*	*Deut 4–11*
a	The call for obedience to God's Torah and cities of refuge (4:41–43)	4:1–43
b	The Ten Commandments ("ten words")	4:44–6:3
x	The Great Commandment—to love God	6:4–9:29
b´	The stone tablets ("ten words") and the Ark of the Covenant	10:1–10
a´	God's requirement of Israel: "to fear Yahweh" (10:12)	10:11–11:25
X	*Covenant Stipulations—the Deuteronomic Code of Law*	*Deut 12–26*
a	Worship at the central sanctuary—centralization of worship	12:1–14:21
b	Periodic duties (including festivals) and concern for the poor	14:22–16:17
x	Leadership in ancient Israel	16:18–18:22
b´	Cities of refuge, holy war, sexual relations	19:1–25:19
a´	Worship at the central sanctuary—presentation of first fruits	26:1–19
B´	*Covenant Ceremonies in Moab and Shechem*	*Deut 27–30*
a	The writing of the Torah on plastered stones and the offering of sacrifices	27:1–10
b	Blessings and curses at the future covenant renewal (Shechem)	27:11–26
x	Covenant renewal—blessings and curses pronounced in Moab	28:1–68
b´	An appeal for covenant faithfulness	29:1–29
a´	The call to decision: life and blessing and death and cursing	30:1–20
A´	*Looking Forward to the Eisodus into Cisjordan*	*Deut 31–34*
a	Deposition of the Torah and appointment of Joshua	31:1–29
b	Song of Moses	31:30–32:47
x	Impending death of Moses	32:48–52
b´	Moses' Testamentary Blessing	33:1–29
a´	Moses' death—Joshua succeeds Moses	34:1–12

Study Questions

These study questions are optional and are designed for the student who wishes to go beyond what is required. *Do not send them to the Center for evaluation.*

1. Examine Deut 6:4–9. What great truth does Moses seek to impress upon the people? How was this truth applied?

2. From Deut 13:1–10 and 18:15–22, list as many rules as you can that are given to regulate prophets and prophecy.

3. What spiritual lessons may a follower of Yeshua learn from the life of Moses, as taught in the book of Deuteronomy?

4. In what ways did King Solomon violate the "law of the king" in Deut 17:14–20?

5. In what ways does the so-called "Outer Frame" of Deuteronomy (chaps. 1–3 and 31–34) function as the introduction to the book of Joshua?

6. What do you think the "sin of Moses" was that prevented him from entering the Promised Land?

Answers to Concept Checks

1. By the Primary History we mean the books of Genesis through 2 Kings in the Tanakh (Hebrew Bible). The center of this structure is found in Exodus 33 (see the 3rd level menorah pattern on page 2), where Moses ascends Mount Sinai to receive a second copy of the Ten Commandments after the incident with the Golden Calf (Exodus 32). As we will see in the next chapter, the account of Moses' conversation with God there, in which he is allowed a glimpse of Yahweh's glory from the protection of a cave on the mountain (Exod 33:12–23), is the center of the Primary History.

2. The center of Genesis 1–11 has to do with the Great Flood in the time of Noah, and the sin of the "sons of God" with the daughters of "Adam" in Gen 6:1–4. The story of the Great Flood reaches its climax in a "new creation"—when God's command to Adam and Eve (Gen 1:28) is repeated to Noah and his family to "be fruitful and multiply, and fill the earth" (Gen 9:1). The central message of Genesis 1–11 is that God has provided a way for human beings to go back to the "Garden of Eden" and the original purposes of creation. Like Enoch and Noah, each one of us has the privilege of "walking with God," if we so choose.

3. As the mother of Ishmael, Hagar has the honor of starting the narrative sequence of the Matriarchs in the book of Genesis. Hagar is the mother of Ishmael, who is included in the covenant of circumcision between God and Abraham (Genesis 17). Ishmael is also the father of twelve "princes" among the Arab descendants of Abraham, the "father of a multitude of nations" (Gen 17:5). Hagar is the only woman in Genesis to whom God communicates directly on two different occasions. As an Egyptian, Hagar functions along with Asenath the Egyptian wife of Joseph, to make a literary framework around the more familiar Matriarchs of biblical tradition: Sarah, Rebekah, Leah and Rachel.

4. Genesis 1–11 and the book of Jonah are not independent literary texts. Either the author of the book of Jonah knew the text of Genesis 1–11 or vice versa. My personal belief is that the author of the story of Jonah composed his work with the structure of Genesis 1–11 in mind. When we understand this, we are in a position to explain the implied ending of the story in terms of the Sabbath rest of Gen 2:1–4.

5. Different stories in Genesis can be taken as the center of the book depending on the questions asked of the text and the particular structure on which we focus our attention. The story of the "binding" of Isaac in Genesis 22 (the *Akedah*) functions as both the concluding episode in the Abraham narrative cycle and as a center of Genesis. Isaac's blessing of his sons Jacob and Esau in Gen 27:1–29 is the center of Genesis in terms of the "Pentateuchal Structure of Genesis." God chose Israel (i.e., Jacob) as a special people through whom he would accomplish the blessing promised to Abraham (Gen 17:5–8), which is for "all the families of the earth" (Gen 12:3). The story of the *Akedah* foreshadows the way in which God accomplishes that blessing through the sacrificial death of Yeshua the Messiah (Jesus Christ).

6. Probably not, because it would lead to confusion. The word "tetrateuch" is already fixed in the literature, within the main stream of biblical scholarship, as referring to the books of Genesis through Numbers. We will probably have to come up with another term to designate the four books of Exodus through Deuteronomy as a literary unit within the Torah, perhaps the "Moses Story."

7. Like Moses, the people of Israel were chosen by God and called to be a servant people. They resisted that call and only reluctantly assumed the role of leadership. Moses was not permitted to enter the Promised Land, though he was given a glimpse of what God had in store for his chosen people. The great prophets of Israel, particularly Isaiah, saw what God had in mind for his servant people Israel—as a light to the nations; but the people of Israel did not enter that "promised land" (i.e., the Kingdom of God). They saw it from a distance, like Moses on Mount Nebo, but they did not experience it as a present reality. It took another "Joshua" (i.e., Yeshua the Messiah) to guide the people of God into the "Promised Land"—to make them into a true light to the nations.

8. It always has been; for that is what the observance of the Eucharist, the celebration of the "Lord's Supper," is all about. At the same time, the familiar Jewish version of the Passover celebration is also finding its way back into Christian worship services in some places—particularly the Passover Seder. The sharing of this experience on the part of Jews and Christians would certainly open the door to deeper dialogue.

9. Yes, they are. Jesus made it clear that he had not come to "abolish the Torah." In fact, his preaching on the Ten Commandments, as preserved in the Sermon on the Mount (Matt 5:17–48), is an attempt to recover the original meaning of these texts in the face of legalism within Jewish circles of interpretation in his day. The law was never the means to salvation. In both the First Testament and the Second Testament, salvation is by faith and faith alone. The Torah was revealed in times past as the "word of God." It remains such—for Christians as well as Jews.

10. Joshua is the link to connect the two phases of the wars of Yahweh—the Exodus from Egypt under Moses' leadership and the Eisodus (Entry) into the Promised Land, which follows. From a literary perspective, the presence of Joshua in the structural center of the Primary History (Exod 33:11) and the transfer of leadership to Joshua in Deuteronomy 34 constitute an envelope around the body of literature we call the first phase of the wars of Yahweh. The reference to Joshua here also functions as an introduction to the second phase, which begins in the first chapter of the book of Joshua.

11. The symbolism of the Tabernacle plays an important role in shaping the architecture of the Temple of Solomon, the Temple of the New Jerusalem as envisioned by the prophet Ezekiel, and the Second Temple in Jerusalem. Moreover, as we will see in a subsequent study of the Epistle to the Hebrews, some knowledge of the architecture and worship in the Tabernacle of ancient Israel is indispensable to understand parts of the Second Testament as well.

12. Very little. Exactly one month passed from the completion of the Tabernacle (Exod 40:17) to the command given to Moses to "keep the Passover at its appointed time" (Num 9:2). Immediately after the observance of that Passover celebration at Mount Sinai, the people departed on their long journey through the wilderness. The events recorded in the book of Leviticus are not dated and are not to be assigned to this single month. They must be assigned to various points in time during Israel's year-long stay at Mount Sinai (in the book of Exodus) and the forty years on the edge of the Promised Land that follows (in the book of Numbers).

13. The content of Leviticus differs much in style from that of Exodus and Numbers, which continue the narrative account of a continuous story. Leviticus presents a static picture of the living cult of the people of Israel. The book of Numbers presents the cultic laws of

the camp in motion. Since the transport of the sacred paraphernalia of worship in ancient Israel and its protection from the encroachment of impurity is the function of the Levites, it is no accident that all the cultic laws pertaining to the Levites are found in Numbers, and none in Leviticus.

14. The destruction of the Third Temple (King Herod's Temple) by the Romans in 70 CE rendered obsolete the basic system of sacrifice and purification on which the priestly regimen of biblical religion rested. Prayers, blessings, readings from the Bible and other sacred texts, observance of the festivals within the synagogue communities, observance of the Sabbath, and observance of "kosher" food laws within individual homes took on new meaning. Though some Jewish movements have altered their liturgy to avoid references to the restoration of sacrifice, it should be noted that Jewish religion has never renounced sacrificial worship permanently.

15. Both Jonah and the people of Israel are justifiably angry for being "swallowed up" by monsters beyond their control. That anger, however, is a great evil—if it excludes compassion for the object of that anger. Atonement focuses on the renewal of sin and guilt so that a holy God and an unholy people may enjoy communion. More than anything else, it is unresolved or misdirected anger that exacerbates the broken relationship between God and human beings. Twice Jonah is asked, "Do you do well to be angry?" (4:4, 9). The answer to that question is a resounding No! The way to "at-one-ment" with God is the way of forgiveness, or "compassion," and not anger.

16. The chapters after the second census in Numbers 26 differ sharply from what precedes. Up to that point the narrative murmuring, rebellion, and death are prevalent. Afterwards the focus is on the fidelity of a new generation, which as a reward does not lose a single life, even in battle (31:49).

17. The wars of Yahweh were remembered and experienced within the community of faith in ancient Israel in public worship. The people came together each year at Gilgal in the spring festival called Passover to reenact the Exodus/Eisodus story in a ritual conquest. They called that story the wars of Yahweh. In similar manner, when Christians celebrate the Eucharist they are remembering the death of Yeshua, which is commemorated in public worship. The Levites in ancient Israel were the guards of the Tabernacle with the twelve tribes assembled in assigned positions around the Tabernacle, as the hosts of Yahweh engaged in "holy war."

18. Mount Hor is the traditional site of Aaron's death and burial, when Eleazar succeeded his father Aaron as high priest (Num 20:23–29). Aaron and Moses both died as punishment for the Meribah incident (Num 20:12–13). Moses died on Mount Nebo, six months after Aaron, and was buried there (Deut 34:5–6). Mount Hor is thus parallel to Mount Nebo in the narrative tradition of ancient Israel. The forty years in the wilderness are divided into two journeys: from Mount Sinai to Mount Hor (and the death of Aaron); and from Mount Hor to Mount Nebo (and the death of Moses). Miriam, Aaron, and Moses all die in the fortieth year after the Exodus from Egypt.

19. Mount Nebo is where Moses was permitted to see the whole of the Promised Land before he died and was buried by God in its vicinity. The death of Moses and the transfer of leadership to his successor Joshua marks the beginning of the second phase of the wars of Yahweh, or what we call here the Eisodus (Entry) into the land of Canaan.

20. Since the only quotation we have from the "Book of the Wars of Yahweh" is in the form of archaic Hebrew poetry, it seems likely that the work in question was a well-known epic poem (like that of the Odyssey or Iliad in ancient Greece). As such, it was probably never actually reduced to written form, other than its use to shape the contents of the Torah as we now have it. In short, the work was not a "book" in the formal sense of that word, or even a scroll. It was an epic poem that was transmitted orally within the religious tradition of ancient Israel. It was probably sung by professional singers (the Levites) who taught it to the people of Israel within the context of the annual pilgrimage festivals.

21. The concept of a "master editor" of the Primary History suggests that there is a difference between the role of author and editor of the Torah. If Moses is considered the author of the five books of the Torah, he is not the author of every word in those books. Like the account of his death and burial, which was not written by Moses, so there are other texts within Exodus, Leviticus, Numbers and Deuteronomy that reflect the hand of a much later editor. That editor has a hand in the writing of the account of David and Bathsheba (2 Samuel 11) and the story of Ahab, Jezebel and Naboth's vineyard (1 Kings 21). And of course, that editor included material on the destruction of Jerusalem by Nebuchadnezzar and the Babylonian Exile in the concluding chapters of 2 Kings.

22. While the book of Deuteronomy is the fifth book of the Torah, it is also the introduction to the Former Prophets (Joshua through 2 Kings). It is thus a literary bridge, which functions as a connecting link between the Torah and the Former Prophets in the canon of the Tanakh (Hebrew Bible)—and the other two sections as well (the Latter Prophets and the Writings).

23. In the period of the Second Temple in ancient Israel the Levites appear as temple singers. The comment that Deuteronomy was in the hands of the Levites suggests that the book was originally transmitted as a musical composition in which the Levites transmitted the performance of the text in an elaborate system of hand signs, called chironomy. This system of notation has come to us in the form of a complex accentual system of marks above and below the Hebrew text in handmade manuscripts. Eventually this living tradition was reduced to a system of written notation by scribes (called the Masoretes) who were far removed in time from the original setting that produced the music of the Bible. If Deuteronomy was composed to be sung or chanted in public worship, then the original Hebrew text is much more like poetry in its rhythmic form than the prose most readers assume it to be.

24. The "Principle Commandment" appears in Deut 6:4—"You shall love Yahweh your God with all your heart, and with all your soul, and with all your might." It is called the "Principle Commandment," or the "Great Commandment," because of the words of Yeshua (Jesus). When asked the question, "Which commandment is the first of all?", he responded by quoting Deut 6:4–5.

25. People in ancient Israel identified blood and suet (fat) as the substances essential for all animal life, including that of human beings. Because they embodied life, the law allotted both blood and suet (fat) to God who was popularly believed to require them as food. Holiness itself was at steak in matters pertaining to blood, which was employed in purification rituals. The vital power of blood helps to explain it widespread uses in purification and consecration in ancient Israel.

26. Kings in the ancient Near East normally had absolute power and often were considered to possess divine attributes, if not divinity itself. According to the law of the king in Deut 17:14–20, the king in Israel was under the authority of the Torah the same as anyone else. Moreover, the king was ordered to have a copy of the Torah, which he was to read, "diligently observing all the words of this law and these statutes" (17:19). The commands that the king not place his trust in military, political, and economic power and to answer to a written code of law essentially forbids the king in Israel to function in the manner of kingship elsewhere in the ancient Near East.

27. Mount Gerizim and Mount Ebal are located on either side of the city of Shechem, which is associated with the renewal of the Mosaic covenant in ancient Israel (see Josh 24:1–28). According to Deut 27:12–13, six of the tribes of Israel assembled on Mount Gerizim to proclaim the covenant blessing and six tribes on Mount Ebal to proclaim the curses within the covenant renewal ceremony. Reference to this covenant ceremony on these two mountains appears at the end of Deut 11 and the beginning of Deut 27 to form a connecting link between these two chapters.

28. The *Nequdoth* in Deut 29:29 are a series of unusual dots over ten successive consonants in the Hebrew text in the Leningrad Codex (and twelve such dots in the Aleppo Codex). They constitute the tenth and final instance of this phenomenon in the Torah. There is dispute among biblical scholars as to the precise meaning of these mysterious marks. The suggestion presented here is that the marks are used to call attention to secret and revealed things—and to the fact that the book of Deuteronomy is in essence an expansion of the original "Ten Words" (the Ten Commandments).

29. Moses did not experience old age in the manner of ordinary human beings. At the time of his death, "his eye was not dim, nor his natural force abated" (34:7). There is nothing recorded in the biblical text to indicate that he had aged. He died because he reached his allotted limit of 120 years. Deuteronomy concludes with the note that there is no one to whom we can compare Moses: "there has not arisen a prophet in Israel like Moses, whom Yahweh knew face to face" (34:10). Unlike other human beings, Yahweh buried him in secret—and "no one knows the place of his burial to this day" (34:6).

30. The pattern achieved in verse count in the Central Core (Deut 12–26) and in word count for the eleven Parashoth and the book of Deuteronomy as a whole is astounding. One could choose to explain this data as evidence of God's handiwork in terms of a supernatural act. If one prefers to explain the data on a human level, the achievement remains difficult to explain in detail. The human effort needed to achieve these totals is almost beyond belief. The only possible explanation is that this is a supreme effort of worship itself—done to the glory of Yahweh.

The BIBAL™ Study Program

The *BIBAL Study Program* is designed to help students achieve fluency in the use of the Bible. The program operates on two levels:

♦ For members of Christian churches, Jewish communities, and the general public who want to improve their understanding of the Bible for ministry and/or personal spiritual growth

♦ For students in the academic community who wish to earn credit toward the completion of an undergraduate degree

The eight courses in the *BIBAL Study Program* are offered in weekend seminars at various locations throughout the year, and on a continuing basis as directed studies, through the Institute of International Studies (IIS).

A. Certificate of Basic Bible Knowledge

Those who complete the two foundational seminars and six core courses (for a total of 24 units) in the *BIBAL Study Program* will earn the *Certificate of Basic Bible Knowledge*.

1. Two Foundational Seminars

Bible 101: Introduction to the Bible (3 units)

An introduction to the Bible which includes 1) a summary of the content of the Bible in its historical and geographical context; 2) the Bible's development from ancient manuscripts to modern translations; 3) analysis of various Bible study tools and methods; and 4) the nature of revelation and inspiration.

Bible 102: The Bible as a Whole (3 units)

An historical study of the development of the canon of sacred Scripture from the time of Moses and the Ten Commandments, to the death of John (96 CE), the last of the twelve disciples of Yeshua (Jesus). The structure, content and unity of the Bible are shown in terms of the ancient Jewish concept of *Tanakh* (= Torah + Prophets + Writings), with the Christian Bible emerging in the hands of John as the "Completed Tanakh."

2. Six Core Courses

Bible 110: Bible Survey—Old and New Testament (3 units for each course = 18 units)

A survey of the First Testament and the Second Testament in six parts (see description of these six courses below). Emphasis is placed on literary structure and the content of each book in the Bible, with emphasis on major themes, broad divisions, key scriptures, and major personalities. The historical and literary backgrounds of all the books in the Bible are covered.

THE BIBAL™ STUDY PROGRAM

1. The Torah (3 units)

When Yeshua (Jesus) said he did not come to destroy "the Law (*Torah*) and the Prophets," he was referring to the foundational Scriptures of God's chosen people. This course shows how important *The Torah* (i.e., the "Five Books of Moses," sometimes called the Pentateuch or the *Chumash*) is for the values and hopes Christians and Jews have in common.

2. The Former Prophets (3 units)

The Former Prophets (Joshua, Judges, 1–2 Samuel and 1–2 Kings) are usually called "History Books" by most Christians. Learn why Yeshua (Jesus) and the first generation of Christians included these books among the "Prophets" and how they relate to the Latter Prophets.

3. The Latter Prophets (3 units)

The Latter Prophets (Isaiah, Jeremiah, Ezekiel, and the Twelve Minor Prophets) stand at the structural center of the Tanakh (Hebrew Bible), which Yeshua (Jesus) and the early Christian Church read and interpreted in terms of God's mission to the nations through his chosen people. This course covers a major part of the First Testament.

4. The Writings in the Tanakh (3 units)

The Writings make up a third collection of books, which was added to the Torah and the Prophets. This course shows how important these books are for understanding the Second Testament and for strengthening faith and hope in difficult times.

5. Apostolic Writings I—the Gospels and Acts (3 units)

How does the story of the Gospels and Acts relate to the "Torah, Prophets, and Writings" (Tanakh)? This course reveals how Israel's hopes for the future were renewed and reinterpreted through the advent of Yeshua (Jesus) and the Spirit-inspired mission of His followers.

6. Apostolic Writings II—New Testament Epistles and Revelation to John (3 units)

How do Paul's letters and those of James, Peter, John, and Jude relate to each other and to the story told in the Gospels and Acts? What is the message of the Revelation to John? This course highlights how this literature enriches the lives of those who seek to live in the light of the biblical story.

For further information on the *BIBAL Study Program*, contact Dr. Duane Christensen directly at:

Institute of International Studies

845 Bodega Way, Rodeo, CA 94572

510-377-7000 (office: cell phone)

801-650-9283 (fax)

510-799-0858 (home)

E-mail: dlc@bibal.net

www.bibal.net

For information on BIBAL Press publications, see the Secure Website
www.dfscott.com

B. Requirements and Procedures

There are five lessons in each of the six Core Courses of the *BIBAL Study Program*. The textbooks include the complete set of lessons for the six core courses. Each lesson includes a chapter on that topic with concept checks, and study questions. The individual chapters, with concept checks, develop the lesson content. The study questions are optional and designed for the student who wishes to go beyond what is required.

Reading the Bible
Reading the entire Bible through is an essential part of the *BIBAL Study Program*. You are required to sign a Reading Report after completing each of the six Core Courses in order to verify the accomplishment of this assignment.

The purpose of the reading is to obtain overall comprehension of the contents. Read rapidly. Do not slow down and get involved in the details. Skimming through sections of detail (in Exodus, Leviticus, etc.) is expected. Try to read as rapidly as possible while still maintaining the sense of what you are reading.

Study Questions
At the end of each lesson in the six Core Courses of the *BIBAL Study Program*, you will find a list of Study Questions. The questions are intended to help you interact with the biblical material as you read it. You may want to read through the discussion questions before you begin your reading in the Bible. Do not send your responses to these questions to the Institute of International Studies (IIS) for evaluation, because they do not comprise any portion of your grade.

The Exams (optional)
There are eight exams in the *BIBAL Study Program*, one after each of the eight individual courses. The exams are made up of 100 questions each (true/false and multiple choice). The exams are open-book. Students are expected to make use of their Bibles and the course texts in answering the exam questions.

Graduating with Honors
The exams and grading in the *BIBAL Study Program* are optional. The exams are designed to assist you in the learning process of the material covered. You may earn the *Certificate of Basic Bible Knowledge* without taking the exams, if you so choose, by simply attending the eight seminars and submitting the required Reading Reports upon completion of each course. It is highly recommended, however, that you decide to take the exams and earn the *Certificate of Basic Bible Knowledge* "with honors," as follows:

THE BIBAL™ STUDY PROGRAM

Summa cum laude	Grade average = 96–100
Magna cum laude	Grade average = 90–95
Cum laude	Grade average = 80–89
With honors	Grade average = 65–79

Assignments for the BIBAL Study Program:

1. Read through each of the five books in the Torah in a single sitting, if at all possible. Read rapidly without getting involved in the details. Focus your attention on maintaining the sense of the whole.

2. Read the appropriate chapter of this textbook.

3. Concept Checks: Answer all the concept check questions and compare your answers to the key which starts on page 119.

4 Answer the Study Questions found at the end of each chapter, if you desire, as a means of digging deeper into the material presented here. *Remember your answers are not to be sent to the center.*